PROJECT
GRIDDLE

Also by
STEVEN RAICHLEN

The Barbecue! Bible®

Project Fire

Project Smoke

Beer Can Chicken

The Brisket Chronicles

Planet Barbecue!

BBQ USA

How to Grill

How to Grill Vegetables

Man Made Meals

Barbecue Sauces, Rubs, and Marinades—
Bastes, Butters, and Glazes, Too

Barbecue! Bible® Best Ribs Ever

Indoor! Grilling

Miami Spice

PROJECT
GRIDDLE

The Versatile Art of Grilling on a Flattop

Steven Raichlen

Workman Publishing
New York

Workman
Workman Publishing
Hachette Book Group, Inc.
1290 Avenue of the Americas
New York, NY 10104
workman.com

Workman is an imprint of Workman Publishing, a division of Hachette Book Group, Inc.
The Workman name and logo are registered trademarks of Hachette Book Group, Inc.

Design by Becky Terhune
Cover photo by Randazzo & Blau

The publisher is not responsible for websites (or their content)
that are not owned by the publisher.

Workman books may be purchased in bulk for business, educational, or promotional use.
For information, please contact your local bookseller or the Hachette Book Group
Special Markets Department at special.markets@hbgusa.com.

Library of Congress Cataloging-in-Publication Data is available.
ISBN 978-1-5235-2887-5

First Edition April 2025

Printed in China on responsibly sourced paper.

10 9 8 7 6 5 4 3 2 1

TO BARBARA,
The sizzle on my griddle,
the wind beneath my wings

CONTENTS

INTRODUCTION

This book began with a very expensive steak. An A5 Wagyu—one of those hyper-rich cuts from Japan that is so extraordinarily well marbled, it looks like white lace over a red tablecloth. To cook it the way I've handled steak for twenty-five years—on the grill over a hot fire—would have sparked a conflagration. Instead, I used the method favored by Japanese chefs for decades: cooking on a hot metal griddle known as a *teppan*. (Think the cooktops at Benihana.) I seared the outside to an audible crunch, while leaving the center of the steak moist and luscious. It was simply one of the best steaks I had ever cooked. (You can read about it on page 140.)

The Japanese aren't the only ones to cook on hot metal slabs. The Spanish have built a sophisticated cuisine around flat metal cooktops known as *planchas*. Argentineans call them *chapas*. Asian comedian-turned-restaurateur Wu Zhaonan invented a version he called the *Mongolian grill*, and used it to launch a culinary empire. In the US, they're simply *griddles* or *flattops*, and we use them to cook bacon and eggs for breakfast; grilled cheese and muffulettas for lunch; chicken under a brick, pork chops, and fried rice for dinner; and medianoche sandwiches for a midnight snack.

Inspired by the sheer deliciousness of my A5 Wagyu, I began to cook other foods on my standing griddle. Breakfast foods you simply can't cook on a traditional grated grill (eggs over easy, anyone?). International classics that theoretically can be grilled but are easier to cook and taste fantastic on a flattop (case in point, tostadas and quesadillas). Fragile foods, like flounder fillets (challenging to cook on a conventional grill). Small foods, like shrimp, that are tedious to grill and even smaller foods that are impossible to grill, like fried rice. And foods you'd never dream of grilling—from latkes to crêpes—that actually taste phenomenal hot off the griddle. Over the past year, I've been firing up my flattop griddle more and more—often in conjunction with my standard grill.

But let's back up a moment. I'm not the only one to have had a griddle epiphany. In 2008, inspired by the Fourth of July breakfasts put on by the local Lions Club in Logan, Utah, entrepreneur Roger Dahle designed a standing outdoor griddle fueled by propane and mounted in a cart, like a gas grill. He named it after his favorite local restaurant (now defunct), and the Blackstone griddle grill was born. More recently, two giants of the barbecue industry—Traeger and Weber—jumped into the standing griddle/flattop grill market—the former with its rugged Flatrock, the latter with both standing griddles and griddle inserts.

Griddles, flattops, planchas, and teppans will never replace outdoor grills, but they offer many advantages that account for their soaring popularity:

- The surfaces are big. You can cook a lot of food on them. In fact, you can cook a whole meal on them (see the Griddle Feasts throughout the book to find out how).

- Griddles are versatile. You can use them to cook every major food group, from dairy to meat to veggies to sweets.

- Griddles are easy to clean and maintain. No grill grates to scour or multiple pots and pans to wash and dry. Just scrape the griddle clean, re-oil it, and you're ready for the next meal.

- Griddles are fast. They heat in a matter of minutes.

- Griddles enhance flavor. The close contact of the food with the hot metal triggers the Maillard reaction, with all its flavor-boosting caramelization of animal proteins and plant sugars. (More on that on page 6.)

- Griddles reduce fat. You use a fraction of the oil for griddling that you do for sautéing or deep-frying.

- Griddles are safe: no open flame or flare-ups—no more explosive ignition or singed arm hair or eyebrows.

- Griddles are stick resistant—perfect for cooking delicate or stick-prone foods, like fish fillets, French toast, or eggs over easy—provided that the griddle is properly seasoned. (More on that on page 14.)

- Griddles reduce waste. There are no gaps like there are between the bars of a grill grate, meaning no more shrimp or asparagus sacrificed to the fire.

And thanks to the advent of the standing griddle, you can now cook outdoors a huge repertory of food once possible to prepare only in your kitchen. I like to think of these griddles as the alter ego to grills. I now have and use both in my outdoor kitchen.

Okay, I hear murmurs of discontent from some of my diehard grill fans. No, Steven Raichlen has not turned his back on grilling. The fact is that while you can grill almost everything, there are many—make that legions—of foods that simply cook and taste better prepared on a griddle.

Lucky for us barbecue buffs, I have developed a technique that combines grilling and griddling—a method I call smoke-griddling and that I use often at home. In a nutshell, you position a portable griddle on a charcoal grill, adding wood chips to the fire. The charcoal heats the griddle, with the resulting woodsmoke perfuming the food. The result could be thought of as barbecue on the griddle—and I've used it with great success on everything from salmon to steak. (More on that on page 18.)

TEN LESSONS I LEARNED AS A TEPPAN YAKI CHEF-IN-TRAINING

Cooking on a plancha, griddle, or teppan is easy—in a sense, easier than grilling. But doing it well requires mastering some essential techniques and a new way to think about cooking. Read about my evening as a teppan yaki chef-in-training on page 174. Here are ten lessons I learned from the experience.

1. Be organized. Have all your ingredients cut, measured, and arranged on trays by dish before you start.

2. Oil your griddle often, and clean it even more often.

3. Use this five-step process for cleaning: Wipe the hot griddle with a dry cotton cloth. Then wipe it with a thickly folded damp cloth. (Work quickly, lest the water in the cloth turn to steam, burning your fingers.) Scrub the griddle with a metal screen, or scrape it clean with a griddle scraper (see Griddle Gear on page 10). Then wipe it with a clean cloth. Oil and wipe it again.

4. After cooking, scrape the griddle clean with a griddle scraper or paint scraper (the kind fitted with a razor blade).

5. Use your oil (safflower oil—prized for its high smoking point) sparingly. Put it in a squeeze bottle and squirt a few squiggles onto the griddle, then spread it with the flat blade of your spatula. Note: Position your squeeze bottle well away from the hot metal cook surface, or you'll melt the plastic. (I learned this the hard way.)

6. When cooking steak, grease the griddle with a piece of steak or other beef fat. (Or bacon fat—why not?)

7. Set up your griddle so you have higher heat in the center (or on one side) and less heat on the periphery. Control the cooking temperature by moving the food closer to or farther away from the high zone.

8. Cut your vegetables thick (¼ inch/6 mm) and your meats thin (½ inch/1 cm). This keeps your veggies crisp in the center and allows your meats to cook through in a matter of minutes.

9. Use a griddle dome to speed up the cooking. Don't have a griddle dome? Use an inverted metal bowl.

10. Have fun and don't forget to smile. Remember, you're the performer and the griddle is your stage.

WHAT IS A GRIDDLE AND WHERE DID IT COME FROM?

Merriam-Webster defines *griddle* as "a flat stone or metal surface on which food is baked or fried." Wikipedia elaborates further: "a cooking device consisting mainly of a broad, usually flat cooking surface. Nowadays it can be either a movable metal pan- or plate-like utensil, a flat heated cooking surface built into a stove or kitchen range, or a compact cooking machine with its own heating system attached to an integrated griddle acting as a cooktop." Whew!

The operative words here are *broad*, *flat*, and *heated*. Thanks to its large surface area, you can cook a lot of food quickly on a griddle, which is why it's the kitchen focal point at breakfast joints, diners, and luncheonettes. The smooth flat surface makes it ideal for cooking foods in semi-liquid form, such as eggs, as well as delicate or stick-prone foods, like fish. For most of human history, griddles were fire heated—first by wood, then by charcoal, and now by propane or electricity.

Etymology buffs may wish to note that, according to the *Oxford English Dictionary* (OED), the word *grydel* first appears in the English language in 1352—as a device for cooking flatbread. A 1430 cookbook, the *Liber Cure Cocorum*, calls for lamprey (eel) to be "rost . . . on gredyl." (Curiously, the book's recipes are written in rhyme!) In 1450, another cookbook cited by the OED extols the virtues of "haddoke . . . yerosted on a gridel." So even back then, griddles were prized for cooking fish— a benefit we appreciate to this day.

Tracing it back further, our word *griddle* seems to come from the Old French *gredil*, which in turn comes from the Latin *craticulum*—a gridiron. Thus, griddles and grills are close etymological cousins—another reason why live-fire fanatics can add griddles to their repertoire with a clean conscience.

GRIDDLES AROUND THE WORLD

Whatever its etymological origins, the griddle's simplicity has made it popular around the planet. At its most elemental, a griddle requires no gas or electrical hookup like a stove. It needs no grate or burner knobs, like a barbecue grill. Simply position it over a heat source (an open wood or charcoal fire will do) and you're ready for business.

Perhaps that explains its ubiquity, for griddles are found on every corner of the globe on every continent. But nowhere is the griddle so deeply embedded in a region's cuisine as it is in Spain, where the plancha does the cooking at humble tapas bars, highfalutin Michelin-starred restaurants, and everywhere in between.

A plancha is a slab of heated metal, and the Spanish use it to cook everything from seafood to steaks to a French toast–like dessert called torrijas (see page 238). The term derives from the Latin *planus*, meaning "flat" or

GRIDDLE, PLANCHA, AND TEPPAN FEASTS

One of the main attractions of griddles—especially the large stand-up kind—is that they enable you to cook a whole meal from start to finish—from starters to desserts—in real time on a single device. Braseros (page 8) take the concept even further, serving as both the cooking device and the dinner table. If you've ever dined at a Japanese steakhouse restaurant, like Benihana, you've witnessed the versatility of the griddle experience. Unlike most cooking equipment, you don't have to cook just a single dish on the griddle. The larger models can produce restaurant-quality meals. In the following pages you'll find a peppering of **Griddle Feasts** (see pages 27, 62, 89, 117, and 227). These are designed to help you use your griddle to the utmost to create rich, full, unforgettable meals.

"smooth"—which is also the origin of the English word *plank*. If you're looking for more plancha street cred, know that Spanish superstar chef and humanitarian José Andrés got his start as the plancha cook (the equivalent of an American short-order cook) at a seafood restaurant on Costa Brava.

Today's griddles are made of metal, but in pre-Columbian times, the Taíno people of what is now Margarita Island in Venezuela cooked on flat clay griddles called *aripos*. If that sounds familiar, you've probably tasted Venezuela's national flatbread: the arepa, which took its name from this clay griddle. (See recipe on page 122.)

Elsewhere in Latin America we find the *budare*—a clay or metal griddle used by indigenous tribes in the Caribbean and northern South America to cook grated manioc root into a crisp flatbread still popular today: cassava bread. Argentineans use round metal cooking plates called *chapas*, counting among their champions the South American grill master Francis Mallmann.

For millennia, Mexicans have cooked tortillas, totopos, and tlayudas on a round, flat clay griddle called a *comal*. Today, most comals are made of metal, but you still find clay and ceramic versions in the Mexican countryside.

On the other side of the Atlantic, cooks in Emilia-Romagna in north-central Italy use a flat ceramic griddle called a *piastra*. (Commercial versions resemble the stainless-steel griddles found at American diners.) On page 124, you'll find a recipe for a sort of Italian quesadilla called *piadina*—traditionally cooked on a piastra.

But it took chefs in Japan to turn griddle cooking into performance art. The year was 1945. The place, a restaurant in the city of Kobe (yes, that Kobe) called Misono, where the cooking was done on a tabletop griddle called a *teppan*. Misono specialized in okonomiyaki, a griddled vegetable pancake, but its postwar patrons, GIs from the United States, craved the beef they were used to eating at home. So chef-owner Shigeji Fujioka took to cooking steaks on his teppan, and teppan yaki (literally "griddle grilling") and the Japanese steakhouse were born.

Misono became a popular restaurant chain in Japan, where the showmanship became as prized as the food. Fast forward to 1964, when Japanese wrestler-turned-restaurateur, Rocky Aoki, opened the first Japanese teppan yaki–style steakhouse in New York. He named it after the flower that serves as the restaurant's logo. Today, Benihana (which means "safflower" in Japanese) has more than sixty-five restaurants across North America.

A similar success story occurred with another style of griddling. Invented by Asian comedian-turned-restaurateur Wu Zhaonan, Mongolian barbecue quickly became a sensation and spread throughout the region, and eventually to the United States. It differs from Japanese teppan yaki in that guests choose the ingredients for their meal from a lavish display of sliced meats (including beef, pork, lamb, chicken, turkey, and seafood), vegetables (broccoli, cabbage, mushroom, onions, and more), and an array of proprietary sauces. Chefs (often more than one) work at a large circular griddle—cooking different meals for different clients simultaneously.

GRIDDLES AND THE MAILLARD REACTION— WHY GRIDDLED FOODS TASTE SO DARN GOOD

Cooking on hot, flat metal fosters the Maillard reaction—named for French physician and chemist Louis Camille Maillard, who was active in the late nineteenth and early twentieth centuries. Maillard was the first to identify the complex chemical reactions that take place when proteins and sugars combine under heat, thereby creating inviting new clusters of colors, aromas, and tastes.

Think of the luscious, smoky, meaty flavors of an expertly seared steak or chicken breast. That's the Maillard reaction at work. Think of the sweet, smoky flavors that arise when you caramelize plant sugars—fried onions, for example, or seared pineapple. That's the Maillard reaction, too.

THE ANATOMY AND TAXONOMY OF THE GRIDDLE

At its most basic, a griddle is a slab or sheet of metal (or sometimes clay or stone). As griddle mania has swept the world, this simple device has evolved into a stand-up cooking center that can rival, in appearance at least, the swankiest gas super grills. In between, there are griddles heated by wood, charcoal, propane, and even electricity. Plus wood-burning griddle-grill hybrids. Here are the most common types.

PORTABLE GRIDDLES

Portable griddles typically measure 20 to 24 inches (50 to 60 cm) long and 15 to 18 inches (38 to 46 cm) wide and are priced under $100. Some have handles at the ends to facilitate moving. Some have grooves or channels inside the edges to gather drippings and fat. Commonly made of cast iron or carbon steel, freestanding griddles can be positioned atop the grate of your barbecue grill, in your pellet grill, over a campfire, or even on your stovetop. Some models are reversible, with a smooth side for griddling and a ridged side to lay on "grill" marks. On the plus side, portable griddles are easy to move and use with virtually any heat source. Their chief drawback is their size—you're limited as to how much food you can cook on them at one time. Portable griddles I like include those made by Lodge and Made In and my own Steven

Raichlen Signature Series griddle. Many grill manufacturers, from Weber to Arteflame to Big Green Egg, make griddle inserts—giving you the best of both worlds in outdoor cooking.

STANDING OUTDOOR GRIDDLES

At first glance, many standing griddles look like barbecue grills, complete with metal cart on wheels, propane tank, burner knobs, and igniter button. You step up to them as you would a gas grill. The lid lifts to reveal a large, flat carbon-steel cooktop heated by gas burners beneath it. The beauty of multiple burners is that they allow you to work over multiple heat zones (see page 16). Another appealing feature of these standing griddles is a hole or slit in the cooktop through which you can scrape grease and food debris into a grease trap below. (Weber's comes with disposable foil liners.) A third advantage is size: Most stand-ups measure 24 to 36 inches (60 to 90 cm) across (there are even 48-inch/120 cm models), which means you can cook whole meals for large numbers of

people on your griddle. But the biggest advantage may be that you can use them outdoors—alongside or in place of your barbecue grill. My griddle stands amid my charcoal grills, smoker, ceramic grill, and wood burner, making it a welcome addition to Raichlen Barbecue Central.

Pioneered by the Utah-based company Blackstone, standing griddles are today manufactured by many of the big grill companies, from Weber to Pit Boss to Traeger. The prices can range from a few hundred dollars to more than $1,000. The European company Evo makes a stylish round stainless-steel griddle that retails for even more.

BUILT-IN AND TABLE GRIDDLES

The rise of the outdoor kitchen has led to the advent of built-in griddles that fit into your counter, for example the Evo Affinity. (Evo makes griddles for both indoor and outdoor kitchens.) Of course, the ultimate built-in griddle is Japan's teppan, in which the metal cooktop actually doubles as the table. For more on teppans, see page 174.

TABLETOP GRIDDLES

Inspired by the teppans of Japan, manufacturers (including Blackstone, Royal Gourmet, and Sophia & William) now sell freestanding electric or gas-fired griddles that sit atop your dinner table. This enables you to have the teppan yaki experience in your dining room—without having to invest in a built-in. These tend to be small and lightweight and do not require special ventilation (according to the manufacturers). They do have limited surface area, but they're a good option for apartment dwellers. Do not attempt smoke-griddling (see page 18) indoors.

BRASEROS

Combine a wood-burning grill with a griddle and you get a *brasero*. Popular in Europe, where it originated, the brasero features a waist-high pedestal surmounted by a round or square metal cooktop with a large aperture in the center. You build a wood fire in the center, which heats the griddle around it. A separate gridiron fits over the hole, enabling you to direct grill as well as griddle. Naturally, the section of the griddle closest to the fire gets the hottest, cooling toward the periphery. So you can actually sit around and eat off a brasero, as you would a patio table, which makes it ideal for entertaining. Well-known braseros available in the US include the Arteflame (made in Cincinnati, Ohio), the OFYR, and the Hancock. Braseros can cost thousands of dollars, but remember, you're buying a grill, a griddle, and an outdoor table (albeit one that may get very hot) all rolled into one.

COMMERCIAL GRIDDLES

You see them in action at your favorite breakfast joint or diner: the large, rectangular stainless-steel griddle that turns out countless bacon and egg breakfasts, BLTs, grilled cheese sandwiches, smash burgers, cheesesteaks, and so on. Gas burners beneath the griddle control the heat, while metal spatulas clatter against the stainless-steel cooktop. You could say the outdoor griddle craze started with these commercial griddles, and as more and more people get into griddling, more of these commercial-style griddles will start turning up in private homes.

WHAT TO LOOK FOR WHEN BUYING A GRIDDLE OR PLANCHA

Plancha and griddle surfaces come in three basic metals: cast iron, carbon steel, and stainless steel. Each has its advantages and drawbacks. (Note: Clay and stone griddles are seldom seen in North America.)

- **CAST IRON** is the most porous of the three, so it's easy to season (treat with vegetable oil or animal fat, like bacon fat—see page 14). Once seasoned, the fat creates a stick-resistant surface—a boon for frying eggs, French toast, and the like. Cast iron spreads heat evenly, making it less likely to burn food over hot spots. The chief disadvantage of cast iron is that when wet or not properly maintained, it rusts. But even here, you can bring back a rusted cast-iron griddle with a little elbow grease. (See page 14.)

- **CARBON STEEL** is denser and harder than cast iron, and somewhat less porous, but nonetheless can be seasoned with oil or animal fat. Its surface tends to be smoother than cast iron. Carbon-steel griddles also spread heat well. But they, too, are prone to rusting when wet or not properly maintained.

- **STAINLESS STEEL** is the metal used to make commercial griddles, high-design griddles, and Japanese teppans. On the plus side, stainless looks sleek and is the smoothest of all three surfaces. The steel itself does not absorb oil, so it has no intrinsic anti-stick properties. It must be oiled conscientiously before each use and scraped clean on a regular basis to prevent the buildup of burnt oil and meat juices. But it doesn't rust, so it's good for restaurants.

- **WHEN BUYING A PORTABLE GRIDDLE, LOOK FOR THICK METAL:** an ⅛ inch (3 mm) is good; ¼ inch (6 mm) is better. The thicker the metal, the more even the heat. Handles make it easy to move the griddle. A well or channel around the periphery of the griddle is useful for capturing fat and meat juices. The Made In Griddle comes 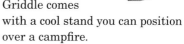 with a cool stand you can position over a campfire.

- **WHEN BUYING A STANDING OUTDOOR GRIDDLE,** look for overall sturdy construction and a lid to cover the cooktop when not in use. Multiple burners give you greater heat control

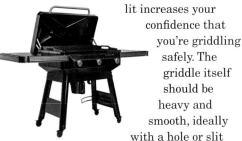

(see box, page 16), while a visible cue that the burners are actually lit increases your confidence that you're griddling safely. The griddle itself should be heavy and smooth, ideally with a hole or slit in one corner or at one edge where you can scrape the excess oil and food scraps. Under this should be a grease trap that's easy to both reach and empty. Extra points for disposable liners you can discard when the grease trap is full. Look for a good, multiyear warranty—since standing griddles live outdoors, they're prone to the same corrosive effects of heat, cold, humidity, and salt air (if you live near the ocean) as gas grills.

- **WHEN BUYING A BRASERO,** look for a cooktop large enough to serve the number of people you normally feed. You also want a heavy-duty grill grate and a vent hole in the firebox to create airflow from both top and bottom. This gives you a hot, clean-burning fire, which makes grilling and griddling a snap. (Lack of such a vent can lead to a smoky, air-starved fire.) Note: The pedestals of many braseros, like the Arteflame, are designed to rust—giving them a handsome weathered appearance. (The steel cook surface does not rust.) No further maintenance required.

GRIDDLE GEAR

One of the many appeals of griddle cooking is that you don't need a lot of fancy equipment. Here are the essentials, plus some helpful extras.

ESSENTIAL TOOLS

METAL SPATULAS: As tongs are to grilling, spatulas are to griddling. They should be heavy duty, with a blade long enough to fit under a steak and wide enough to scoop up a fried egg: 7 to 8 by 3 inches (18 to 20 by 8 cm) is ideal. Holes in the blade prevent the bottom of the food from getting soggy. The handle should be offset, so you don't burn your knuckles.

TONGS: You also want a pair of spring-loaded metal tongs to help move and turn the food.

SCRAPERS: You'll need a scraper for cleaning your griddle. Choose one with a wide head (4 to 6 inches/10 to 15 cm) and a sharply beveled edge. The chefs at Benihana use what looks like a paint scraper affixed with a wide razor blade at the end. (One good brand is Winco.) There's nothing like it for removing burnt-on layers of oil.

TWO-PRONG CARVING FORK: Use this for stirring food on your griddle and for scraping the food off your spatula onto a platter or plate.

GRIDDLE DOME: An inverted bowl–shaped metal dome with a heatproof handle and a small hole on top to release steam. Useful for melting cheese on a burger and cooking thicker or denser foods. Place one on top when frying a sunny-side up egg.

spatula

parchment paper

spatula

griddle press

griddle dome

scraper

spatula

scraper

point-and-shoot thermometer

carving fork

gas gauge

tongs

squirt bottles

insulated gloves

Alternatively, use an inverted metal bowl, wok lid, or a deep disposable aluminum foil pan. Slide the sharp blade of your spatula under one side of the bowl to lift it.

GRIDDLE PRESS: A heavy, round or rectangular plate with a heatproof handle. Some come flat (my favorite); others are ridged to simulate grill marks (not my favorite). These are indispensable for making smash burgers. In a pinch, use the bottom of a cast-iron skillet.

SQUIRT BOTTLES: Use one for oil, a second for water. Squirt thin streams of oil on your griddle, then spread them out with the flat blade of your spatula to grease the griddle. Squirt the water for steam-griddling vegetables (see page 17) and cleaning your griddle while it's still hot.

POINT-AND-SHOOT THERMOMETER: Essential for gauging the precise surface temperature of your griddle. Point the red laser beam at the section you wish to measure; a few seconds later, you'll get a precise temperature reading. I like the Maverick IR-203 Laser Infrared Thermometer.

FOOD-SAFE LATEX GLOVES: Useful for handling raw poultry, meat, seafood, etc.

SUEDE OR LEATHER GRILL GLOVES/ INSULATED GLOVES: Useful for handling hot objects—especially when you use a portable griddle or plancha on a barbecue grill.

GAS GAUGE: There's nothing worse than running out of propane during a griddle session. One good model is the Dozyant Propane Tank Gauge Level Indicator.

PARCHMENT PAPER: Use this nonstick, slow-to-burn paper when griddling thick sandwiches, like muffulettas and Cubanos. (See page 17.)

HELPFUL TOOLS

ALUMINUM FOIL PANS: As they are for grilling, disposable foil pans are a big help for griddling. Use them for carrying ingredients to the griddle and for marinating. Use them for boiling down that marinade to make a sauce while the food cooks. (Place the foil pan directly on the griddle.) I recommend buying at least two sizes: 13 by 9 inches (33 by 23 cm) and 9 by 6 inches (23 by 15 cm). They can also serve as a griddle dome (see page 10).

EGG RING: To help you griddle perfectly round sunny-side up or fried eggs. Grease well. You can also use the well-oiled metal ring of a Mason jar. Position it top side down and crack the egg in the center. When you flip it with a spatula to cook an over-easy egg, the ring will lift off easy.

PANCAKE BATTER DISPENSER: Looks like a metal funnel with a lever for opening the bottom to release the batter. Alternatively, make the batter in a blender (most blenders have spouts), or place it in a large measuring cup with a spout (which is easier to pour from than a bowl).

CRÊPE RAKE: Used for spreading crêpe batter into a thin circle.

SMOKE PUCK (MADE BY YOURS TRULY): Yes, you can actually smoke on a griddle. Fill the smoke puck or other grill-top smoking device with hardwood sawdust or pellets. Place on a hot griddle. When you see smoke (after 3 to 5 minutes), reduce the heat to the desired temperature. Place the food on the griddle, and cover it and the smoke puck with a griddle dome. Note: Use only with outdoor griddles.

WIRE RACK: One advantage of griddling is how it crisps tortillas, salami, cheese disks, and so forth. These items may come off the griddle soft and pliable, but they crisp on cooling—provided air circulates on both top and underneath. Let them cool on a wire rack, like a cake rack, to do the trick.

TOOLS FOR CLEANING

I cannot stress the importance of cooking on a clean griddle. Here's what you'll need for the job (see page 19 for how to do it).

GRIDDLE SCREENS: Fine metal mesh screens for scouring your griddle. Buy a holder with an insulated handle. One good brand is Cusinium.

METAL SCRUBBY: Works well on carbon and stainless steel. It should be soap-free.

PUMICE STONE: You also see these being used for cleaning griddles. They're available online; one good brand is Mowot. Be sure to wipe the griddle with a clean cloth afterward to remove any bits of stone.

CLEAN COTTON CLOTHS: For wiping down the griddle and applying a thin film of oil after use. Make sure the cloth is lint free.

PAPER TOWELS: You'll want plenty of these for cleaning and oiling.

griddle screens

clean cotton cloths

pumice stones

metal scrubbies

paper towels

PREPPING YOUR GRIDDLE FOR FIRST USE

Whether you buy a small portable griddle or a standing gas super griddle, you'll need to clean and season it before using.

Most griddles come from the factory with a protective layer of food grade oil. Scrub it off using a scrub brush and hot soapy water. *This is the last time you'll use soap on your griddle.* Dry it well with paper towels.

SIX STEPS TO SEASONING YOUR GRIDDLE

Seasoning involves a process called polymerization, which is a fancy way of saying chemically combining smaller molecules (called monomers) into larger chains or networks of larger molecules (called polymers)—in this case, forming a thin, shiny coating of oil or grease (like bacon fat) to make the surface of your griddle stick resistant. To further season your griddle, do your first cook with a fatty protein, like bacon or breakfast sausage.

1. To season your griddle, use a folded paper towel held at the end of tongs, dip it into a small bowl of neutral vegetable oil, like canola or safflower oil, and use it to coat the entire surface of the griddle, including the sides. Apply an even, generous coat. Wipe off any excess oil with a clean paper towel.

2. *If using a freestanding griddle or plancha,* place it over a medium-hot heat source (like your barbecue grill or stove). Heat it until the surface starts to smoke and darken, 5 to 15 minutes. You can also heat the griddle in a pellet grill or in a 400°F (200°C) oven. *If using a standing outdoor griddle,* turn the burners on medium-high and heat until the surface starts to smoke and darken.

3. Wearing insulated gloves and using a clean, lint-free cotton cloth or paper towel, wipe off any excess beads or pools of oil. Allow the griddle to cool completely, about 30 minutes.

4. Generously spread the griddle or plancha with a second coat of oil, wiping off the excess. Heat it over medium-high heat again until it starts to smoke and darken, 10 minutes or so.

5. Again, wearing insulated gloves, wipe off any excess beads or pools of oil. Allow the griddle to cool completely, 30 minutes.

6. Oil and heat the griddle or plancha a third and final time. Wipe off the excess oil and again let it cool completely.

Your griddle or plancha should now be dark charcoal gray to black with a smooth, shiny surface. It's properly seasoned and ready for griddling. The best way to keep a griddle seasoned is to use it frequently—the more you use a griddle, the better seasoned it becomes.

Always start by heating and oiling it. Always scrape it clean with a scraper and oil it when you're finished cooking.

At some point, you may heat the griddle too high and burn off the seasoning. (The metal will look bare.) Or you'll leave your griddle out or uncovered and it will get wet. It might even rust. Fear not: It's not ruined. Simply scrape it clean with a scraper. Or in the case of rust, brush it off

Remove rust from a griddle with a scraper and/or metal scrubby or pumice stone (no soap!), then season it a second time.

with a metal scrubby, griddle screen, pumice stone, or steel wool (the soapless variety). If using pumice stone, you need to wipe off the griddle with a clean, lightly oiled cloth to remove any bits of stone. Then reseason it as directed.

FIRING IT UP

You've cleaned and seasoned your new griddle. Now you're ready to fire it up. If using a portable griddle, heat it on your charcoal or gas barbecue grill (or indoors over your stove burners).

Most griddle cooking is done over medium to medium-high heat (350° to 400°F/175° to 200°C). If your griddle is large enough, set up multiple heat zones. This is easy to do on a three- or four-burner gas-fired standing griddle. When using a portable griddle on a gas grill, light a burner under one side and leave the burner off on the other. With practice you'll learn to gauge your griddle's cooking zones.

Check the temperature using a point-and-shoot thermometer (see page 12).

If you don't have one, sprinkle a few drops of cold water onto the plancha with your fingertips.

- If the water evaporates in 1 to 2 seconds, the griddle is hot.

- If it takes 3 to 4 seconds, the heat is medium.

- More than 5 seconds, it's low.

Now oil the griddle. Use an oil with a high burn point, like canola oil, safflower oil, or grapeseed oil. Avoid corn and peanut oil, which tend to leave a gummy residue. I personally like extra virgin olive oil and toasted sesame oil, which, yes, have a lower burn point but provide a flavor dividend in addition to lubrication.

Squirt the oil in squiggles (that's where the squeeze bottle comes in), then spread it around with the flat blade of your spatula. Alternatively, grease your griddle with a folded paper towel dipped in oil, clasped in tongs, and rubbed over the surface.

HEATING YOUR PLANCHA OR GRIDDLE

Different foods require different cooking temperatures. In the recipes in this book, you'll be asked to heat your griddle to high, medium, low, and so on. Here's a guide to the various temperature ranges and the foods for which they're appropriate. Use a point-and-shoot thermometer (see page 12) to gauge the heat.

- **HIGH** (450° to 500°F/230° to 260°C) for searing; good for thin steaks, chops, thin fish fillets, etc.

- **MEDIUM-HIGH** (400°F/200°C) for searing and cooking; good for thicker steaks, chicken breasts, burgers, fish steaks and thicker fillets, vegetables, stir-frying

- **MEDIUM** (350°F/175°C) for cooking; good for sandwiches and breakfast items such as pancakes, French toast, and bacon

- **MEDIUM-LOW** (300°F/150°C) for cooking and warming; good for larger cuts of meat, like bone-in chicken thighs, pork chops, and so on

- **COOL** (250°F/120°C) for warming

- **NO-HEAT** (ambient temperature) for holding food

The advantage of this method is that you clean the griddle while you're oiling it.

Another great way to add flavor is to use butter or a hunk of bacon or beef fat. For butter, impale a 1- to 2-inch (3 to 5 cm) piece on a fork and rub it across the hot griddle. (Remember, butter burns more readily than oil, so don't heat the griddle too high and put the food on immediately after buttering.) Or grease your griddle with a cube of beef or pork fat or a folded strip of bacon held at the end of tongs. Whichever fat type you choose, apply it thoroughly but not wastefully— enough to coat the surface of the griddle where you're cooking but not so much that it puddles and burns. Now you're ready to cook.

GRIDDLE COOKING TECHNIQUES

Most griddling is done in a pretty straightforward manner. You heat the griddle and oil it well. Add the food. Cook until sizzling and browned on the bottom, then cook the other side the same way until done in the center. It's as simple as that. The short list of foods we griddle in this way includes eggs, pancakes, French toast, thin steaks and chops, burgers, chicken breasts, fish fillets, shrimp and crabcakes, thinly sliced vegetables and fruits, noodles, rice, and more. Which isn't such a short list after all.

DIVIDE-AND-CONQUER GRIDDLING

I use this for thick sandwiches, like medianoches and muffulettas (pages 74 and 77, respectively). Build the sandwich in two halves, with the cold cuts on top. Layer a sheet of parchment paper atop the cold cuts, and start griddling the meat with the parchment paper side down. When the meats are hot and sizzling, carefully turn the half sandwich so the bread side is down. Peel off and discard the parchment paper. Put the two halves together and your sandwich is ready.

Dome griddling traps the heat.

STEAM GRIDDLING

This is a technique developed in Asia to facilitate griddling dense vegetables, like broccoli and winter squash. Work over a medium-hot to hot griddle. Start by cooking the vegetables in oil. Then squirt a tablespoon or two of water on the vegetables. It will boil rapidly, steaming the vegetables in the process. Add more water as needed until the vegetables are sizzling and lightly browned. To intensify the effect, place a griddle dome over the food.

Use parchment to griddle sandwiches.

DOME GRIDDLING

Use this method for cooking larger or slower-cooking foods, like thicker steaks and chops, chicken pieces, fish steaks—any food that requires a little more heat and time to cook. Place a griddle dome (page 10) or metal bowl over the food while it's on the griddle to hold in the heat. Use dome griddling for melting the cheese in a grilled cheese sandwich and speeding up the cooking of a sunny-side up egg.

Steam griddling sizzles and steams.

SALT GRIDDLING

A unique method for griddling that Spanish chef José Andrés uses to cook carabineros—Spain's supernaturally succulent scarlet shrimp. (They take their name from the scarlet uniforms once worn by Spanish carabineros, or police.) Spread out coarse sea salt in a ½-inch-thick (1 cm) layer over your plancha. Heat it well, then lay the shrimp on top. Note: The Spanish like their shrimp barely cooked (make that half-raw) in the center.

SMOKE-GRIDDLING METHOD #1

I developed this technique during my first ventures in griddling on a charcoal grill. Rake out the coals in an even layer. Place the griddle on the grill and heat it. Add handfuls of hardwood chips or one or two wood chunks to the fire at the edges. When you see smoke, put the food on the griddle. Close the grill lid to hold in the smoke. This technique is great for poultry, pork, and seafood.

SMOKE-GRIDDLING METHOD #2

In this method, you smoke right on the surface of the griddle. Heat one zone to high and one zone to medium. Mound a handful of hardwood chips or pellets or a couple of tablespoons of hardwood sawdust directly on the griddle over the hot zone. When it starts to smoke, slide the wood to the medium zone and place the food to be griddled next to it (oil it first). Cover with the griddle dome. Griddle the food covered—the smoldering wood will provide a delicate smoke flavor.

Smoke-griddling method #2 uses a dome to capture the smoke.

In Smoke-griddling method #1, wood is added to the fire.

HOW TO CLEAN YOUR GRIDDLE

Okay, you made a great meal and are basking in the appreciation of your guests. You're not done yet. You need to clean and oil the griddle, so it gives you the best possible performance the next time you use it.

Clean your griddle while it's hot. Scrape any excess oil or food debris off your griddle (or into the grease trap). Use a beveled-edge scraper or a razor-blade-type paint scraper.

Should your griddle need additional cleaning—to remove stuck scrambled eggs, for example—scour it with a soap-free metal scrubby. (Wear insulated gloves so you don't burn your hands.)

Another way to dislodge food residue is to squirt the hot griddle with a little water, bring it to a boil, then scour it with the scrubby.

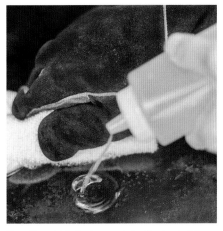

Once the griddle is clean and dry (the heat of the griddle will evaporate the water—you can speed up the process by drying with paper towels or a clean kitchen towel), oil it well, then turn off the heat and let cool. Cover it until the next use.

YOU CAN COOK *WHAT* ON YOUR GRIDDLE?

The uses of your griddle are so varied; the recipes in this book scarcely scratch the surface. Here are some additional foods you may never have realized you can cook on a griddle.

Cheese

Not a grilled cheese sandwich. But coarsely grated cheese sizzled directly on the griddle. Use firm grating cheeses, like cheddar, Parmigiano, Gruyère, Manchego, and so on. Spoon it in mounds 2 to 3 inches (5 to 8 cm) in diameter and cook over medium heat until melted into a flat disk and the fat starts to separate out. (This will take a minute or two—do not overcook.) Using a spatula, transfer the cheese disks to a wire rack. They'll crisp on cooling. See page 50.

Crêpes

The round, gas-heated metal cookers used by crêpe makers in France are nothing more than circular griddles. Pour your favorite crêpe batter onto a medium-hot griddle. Use a crêpe rake (you can order one online) or a large spoon to spread the batter into a large, thin circle. Brown both sides, turning with a spatula— 30 to 60 seconds per side will do it. See recipe on page 243.

Croissants

Croissants taste great. Pressed griddled croissants taste even better. Cut the croissant in half through the side. Griddle over medium-high heat in melted butter or olive oil under a griddle press (or the bottom of a skillet). Cook until browned and crisp, 2 to 3 minutes per side. This endows the croissant with a buttery wafer-crispness.

Noodles

From Japanese yakisoba to Chinese lo mein, noodles taste great cooked on a griddle. Think of the hot metal as a flat wok. Start by searing your aromatics (minced ginger, garlic, scallion) and vegetables (chopped onion, carrot, celery, cabbage, green beans, etc.). Then sear your protein (thinly sliced chicken, beef, pork, shrimp, or tofu). Next, griddle your noodles (cooked soba, lo mein, spaghetti). Stir it all together and add your flavorings—soy sauce, mirin, chili paste, sugar, etc.—and you've got a griddle feast. By the way, the griddle is excellent for reheating leftover spaghetti carbonara and cacio e pepe, and if you work on a hot griddle, you might even get a crisp crust.

Popcorn

Heat your griddle or plancha to high and spread about 1 tablespoon of canola or olive oil in a circle. Place 3 to 4 tablespoons popcorn kernels on the griddle and cover with a griddle dome. The popcorn will pop in 3 to 5 minutes. Lift the dome and transfer the popcorn to a bowl. Season with salt and melted butter. I learned this trick from the folks at Weber.

Onigiri

The Japanese cook these flat cakes of sticky rice on the hibachi. It's even easier on a griddle. The next time you have leftover sticky rice (or sushi rice—it's even more flavorful), form it into hockey puck shapes 3 inches (8 cm) across and ¾ inch (2 cm) tall. Cook these on a medium-hot griddle until crisp and lightly browned on both sides, 2 to 3 minutes per side, carefully turning with a spatula. Sprinkle with black sesame seeds.

Salami chips

Yes, you can griddle salami, pepperoni, prosciutto, and other cold cuts. Work over medium heat and lightly oil the griddle or plancha. Cook until sizzling on the bottom, then invert with a spatula. Transfer the griddled salami or other meat to a wire rack—the chips will crisp on cooling. Munch them out of hand or use as a dipper for guacamole, onion dip, queso fundido, and so on.

Sausages

Prior to joining Planet Barbecue® (my prepared food line) as COO, my stepson Jake Klein ran a gastropub in Brooklyn called Jake's Handcrafted. His sausages were highly innovative (think unexpected flavors like Cubano, Reuben, and Japanese chicken), and he cooked them on a griddle. Heat the griddle or plancha to medium and cover the sausages with a griddle dome. About 4 to 6 minutes per side will do it.

Chicken pieces

One of the most tedious—and messiest—tasks in the kitchen is browning chicken pieces to make fricassees, sautés, and paprikas. Instead, brown the bird over medium-high heat on your griddle or plancha. Not only do you take the mess outside, but the rendered chicken fat is a great way to grease your griddle.

CHAPTER 1

BREAKFAST

Breakfast may not be the first meal you think of when it comes to outdoor cooking. But when many people fire up their griddles for the first time, that's exactly what they cook. Bacon. Eggs. Pancakes. French toast. Or the many other dishes that make the North American breakfast such a joyful, substantial, and belt-loosening meal. Get ready for:

BACON MEETS GRIDDLE

SERVES 2 TO 6

I feel a little awkward dedicating a page of this book to telling you how to prepare bacon. But it's one of the first things you'll cook on your new griddle, and you might as well do it properly. Besides, bacon won't stick to a well-seasoned griddle, and if you work outside, it won't spatter up your stove. A griddle press keeps the strips flat and even and helps speed up the cook time. Note: Pancetta (Italian cured and rolled—but not smoked—pork belly) would be cooked the same way. Did I mention the bacon weave? See the next page.

---

12 to 16 ounces (340 to 455 g) of your favorite bacon (thick-cut or thin-cut)

YOU'LL ALSO NEED
Griddle press (or cast-iron skillet)

---

1. Spread a layer of paper towels on a plate. Arrange the bacon strips on your griddle or plancha. (There is no need to preheat the griddle; in fact, starting with a cold griddle causes less curling. However, if you've already preheated your griddle to cook other foods, such as eggs or toast, you can also start cooking the bacon on a hot griddle. Note that the cooking time may be shorter.) Set the heat on medium and cook the bacon until sizzling and browned on the bottom, 2 to 4 minutes, or as needed. If you like, place a griddle press on top to keep the bacon from curling.

2. Invert the bacon with tongs and cook the other side the same way, continuing to press the bacon to keep it from curling.

3. Transfer the bacon to the paper towel–lined plate to drain. Serve while hot and crisp.

WHAT ELSE Bacon plays such a key role in the American diet (and psyche), most supermarkets devote 4 feet (just over a meter) of shelf space to display it. Unfortunately, not all bacons are equal. In fact, most commercial bacon never sees the inside of a smokehouse. It's injected with smoke flavoring and "cured" in a matter of hours. To enjoy bacon at its best, you want a true smokehouse bacon (one that's smoked with real hardwood). Two good brands are Neuske's and Benton's. So, what's the deal with "uncured bacon"? A few decades ago, in the wake of some sloppy science, sodium nitrite stood accused of being a carcinogen. Sodium nitrite occurs naturally in underground deposits (and in celery) and has been used as a safe curing salt for millennia. It has long since been exonerated, but a prejudice against its use remains. I personally prefer the inviting pink color and rich umami taste of bacon cured with sodium nitrite, but some people still eschew it—hence the popularity of "uncured" bacon. Obviously, it's your call.

WHAT'S MORE Bacon reaches its apotheosis here in a preparation known as the bacon weave. In a nutshell, you weave a package of bacon strips into a square, which you sizzle on your griddle. The resulting sheet—crisp and meaty—makes a great base for toppings. Or place it while still hot and pliant in a taco holder to make a crisp bacon taco shell. Another bonus: You can make the weave ahead of time and store it in the fridge until you're ready to cook it. Here's how to do it.

1. Moisten your countertop with a damp towel. (This keeps the foil and fatty bacon from slipping.) Lay a sheet of aluminum foil (at least 18 by 24 inches/ 46 by 60 cm) flat on the countertop, narrow end parallel to the edge.

2. Make the bacon weave: Start with 16 thin strips of bacon. (Make sure you start with 16 strips. The commonly sold 12-ounce/340 g packages contain only 12 strips.) Lay 8 strips horizontally on the foil, positioning them so their edges touch. From their halfway points (which will be the centerline of the weave), fold back every other strip of bacon, i.e., strips 1, 3, 5, 7, etc. Lay a piece of bacon perpendicular to the fold, making sure it's snug. Unfold the bacon slices over the new strip. Repeat with alternate strips, i.e., strips 2, 4, 6, 8, etc. Continue until the weave is complete and roughly square.

3. Lay a large sheet of plastic wrap over the weave (you may need two sheets) and gently flatten the weave with a rolling pin to tighten and enlarge it. (Thinner bacon also crisps better.) Remove the plastic wrap and invert the bacon onto the griddle, then peel the foil away. Cook the bacon on the griddle as directed in the recipe.

PROSCIUTTO BACON

SERVES 1 (CAN BE MULTIPLIED AS DESIRED)

I dreamed up prosciutto bacon to crown a cheeseburger I created for my Italian TV show, *Steven Raichlen Grills Italy*. I loved the sweet-salty crunch, the umami tang, the sense of eating something familiar, yet so delectably different. This crispy cured ham quickly became a staple at Raichlen cocktail parties. I cooked it on the grill, of course. (At the time, I cooked everything on the grill.) But that preparation presented challenges, not least of which was the tendency of the paper-thin ham slices to burn in the process of crisping. The griddle delivers the same salty crunch in a much more controlled cooking environment.

Thinly sliced prosciutto
(figure on 2 ounces/60 g per person)
Extra virgin olive oil for brushing the prosciutto and the griddle

YOU'LL ALSO NEED
Wire cooling rack

---

1. Heat your griddle or plancha to medium.

2. Lightly brush each prosciutto slice on both sides with olive oil. Oil the griddle.

3. Arrange the prosciutto slices on the griddle. Cook until sizzling, browned, and crisp on the bottom, 1 to 3 minutes.

4. Invert the slices and cook the other side the same way.

5. Transfer the prosciutto bacon to a wire rack and let cool. The slices will crisp on cooling.

WHAT ELSE This recipe calls for prosciutto, but you can cook other of the world's great dry cured hams, from Spanish serrano to Italian speck (smoked prosciutto) the same way.

WHAT'S MORE So how do you use prosciutto bacon? Let me count the ways. Nibble it as you would potato chips. Crumble it on salads. Serve it with scrambled eggs. Pile it on sandwiches. The possibilities are endless.

LUMBERJACK'S BREAKFAST

Let the Italians have their cornetti, the French their croissants. (Okay, legend has it these crescent-shaped pastries were invented by the Austrians to celebrate the defeat of an Ottoman army outside Vienna in 1683.) I raise my fork for the American breakfast—that glorious, plate-burying feast of bacon, eggs, hash browns, pancakes, and more. The griddle both inspired—and perhaps determined—this uniquely American approach to the morning meal. This one is substantial enough to sate even a lumberjack's hunger. So brew a pot of coffee and fire up your griddle. The morning show is about to begin.

Here's what's on the menu:

- Bacon Meets Griddle (page 24)
- Jake's Breakfast Sausage (page 28)
- Smash Browns (aka Smashed Potatoes) (page 209)
- Dirty Fried Eggs (page 31)
- Limoncello Pancakes (page 37)

Here's how to sequence the preparation:

The night before:
- Make the breakfast sausage. Boil the potatoes for the smash browns.

Before the meal prep:
- Make the pancake batter.

The actual cook:
- Heat your griddle or plancha with one zone on medium-high, one on medium, and one low for warming.

- Start by frying the bacon on the medium zone. Move it to the low zone to keep it warm.

- Coat the breakfast sausage in the bacon fat and cook on the medium-high zone. Move it to the low zone to keep it warm. Spread the bacon and sausage fat over the griddle with your spatula (you'll use it to cook the smash browns and dirty eggs).

- Cook the smash browns on the medium-high zone. Slide them to the low zone.

- Cook the dirty eggs on the medium-high zone. Serve them with the bacon, sausage, and smash browns.

- Finally, cook the pancakes on the medium-high zone, adding butter as needed. Serve.

Now *that's* what I call breakfast!

JAKE'S BREAKFAST SAUSAGE

MAKES 4 PATTIES, SERVES 2 TO 4

Most sausage making requires a fair degree of skill. There are stuffers to operate, casings to fill, and links to be twisted and tied. And that's *before* curing and smoking. Breakfast sausage, however, can be made in a matter of minutes with no more special equipment than a wooden spoon and bowl. Just ask Jake Klein. Jake is my partner in Planet Barbecue, LLC—our prepared barbecue company—and before that, he ran Jake's Handcrafted, a sausage and craft beer emporium in Brooklyn. And readers of my previous books will recognize him as my stepson. Fresh thyme and sage make this sausage fragrant, cracked black pepper and hot red pepper flakes notch up the heat, while brown sugar gives it a pleasing hint of sweetness. You can make it from scratch a few minutes before you're ready to serve breakfast. Best of all, the griddle browns the sausage quickly and evenly, keeping the spattering grease off your stove.

---

1 pound (455 g) ground pork

1½ tablespoons dark brown sugar

1 tablespoon chopped fresh sage

1 teaspoon chopped fresh thyme

1 teaspoon hot red pepper flakes

1 teaspoon coarse salt (sea or kosher)

1 teaspoon cracked black peppercorns

YOU'LL ALSO NEED
A griddle dome

---

1. Place the pork in a mixing bowl. Sprinkle the sugar, sage, thyme, red pepper flakes, salt, and cracked peppercorns over the pork. Mix well with a wooden spoon or your hands (if using the latter, wear food-safe gloves).

2. Line a plate with plastic wrap. Form the sausage into 4 equal patties, each about ½ inch (1 cm) thick, and arrange them on top. Cover with more plastic wrap and store in the refrigerator until ready to cook. The patties can be formed up to 24 hours ahead of time—

indeed, the flavor will intensify with age.

3. Heat your griddle or plancha to medium-high.

4. Arrange the sausage patties on the griddle about 2 inches (5 cm) apart and cook until sizzling and browned on both sides, about 2 minutes per side, turning with a spatula. Serve with your favorite eggs, biscuits, etc.

WHAT ELSE You want ground pork with a fairly high fat content: 25 percent is ideal. If you can find pork from a heritage breed, like Berkshire or Mangalitsa, your sausage will be all the more flavorful.

WHAT'S MORE The traditional way to enjoy breakfast sausage in Brooklyn is as an SEC (sausage, egg, and cheese). For bread, use a kaiser roll or English muffin. Butter the cut sides and warm on the griddle. Fry the eggs in the sausage fat. Place a sausage patty on the roll, followed by a slice of American or cheddar cheese. Top with the egg—the heat of the sausage patty and egg will melt the cheese. (Or speed up the process using a griddle dome.) Jake wouldn't say no to using pancakes instead of the bread.

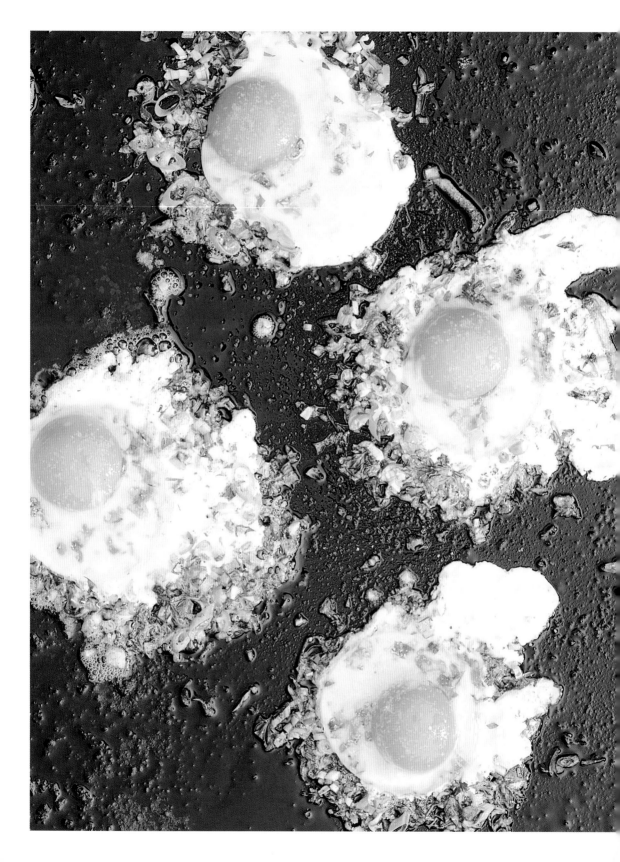

DIRTY FRIED EGGS

MAKES 2 EGGS (CAN BE MULTIPLIED AS DESIRED)

I'm not about to tell you how to cook fried eggs on the griddle. But I will tell you how I make fried eggs that feature a palate-blasting rush of garlic, scallions, chiles, and cilantro.

---

1 clove garlic, peeled and minced

1 scallion, trimmed, white and green parts thinly sliced crosswise

1 jalapeño or serrano chile, seeded and minced (for spicier eggs, leave the seeds in)

3 tablespoons minced fresh cilantro or flat-leaf parsley

2 tablespoons cold unsalted butter in a chunk for the griddle, plus more as needed

2 large eggs (preferably organic)

Coarse salt (sea or kosher) and freshly ground black pepper

YOU'LL ALSO NEED
A griddle dome (optional)

---

1. Place the garlic, scallion, chile, and cilantro in a small bowl and stir to mix.

2. Heat your griddle or plancha to medium-high.

3. Impale the butter on a fork and rub half of it in two 3-inch (8 cm) circles on the griddle. Once the butter is melted and sizzling, spoon the chopped aromatics onto the butter and spread them out to form two 3-inch (8 cm) circles. Cook the aromatics until sizzling and just beginning to color, 20 seconds.

4. Crack the eggs on top of the aromatics. Season with salt and pepper. Fry the eggs until cooked to taste, 2 to 3 minutes for sunny-side up. If you have a griddle dome, cover the eggs to help cook the tops. If you like your eggs over easy, slide a spatula under each egg and move it to the side. Re-butter the griddle and invert the eggs on top of it. Cook an additional minute.

WHAT ELSE For an eggs-and-bacon breakfast, fry the bacon and then cook the eggs in the bacon fat. Serve with Smoked Paprika Garlic Bread, page 120.

WHAT'S MORE Slice the jalapeños paper-thin and cook the eggs over easy for cool-looking dirty eggs embedded with inviting circles of caramelized jalapeños.

BACON AND EGGS IN A HOLE

MAKES 2, SERVES 1 OR 2 (CAN BE MULTIPLIED AS DESIRED)

Here's a breakfast so simple even a child can make it. Indeed, I first learned the recipe in a scouting manual when I was growing up. The preparation rolls a bacon, egg, and toast breakfast into a single dish. It's simple, but it does require a little orchestration so that the toast comes out crisp and the yolk comes out runny (or however you like it). For a meatless version, use butter and/or extra virgin olive oil instead of bacon fat.

2 slices of your favorite bread (each about ½ inch/1 cm thick)

3 tablespoons unsalted butter at room temperature, plus 2 tablespoons cold butter in a chunk for the griddle

4 strips bacon

Extra virgin olive oil for the griddle (optional)

2 large eggs (preferably organic)

Coarse salt (sea or kosher) and freshly ground black pepper

1 tablespoon minced fresh chives or scallion greens (optional)

YOU'LL ALSO NEED

A griddle dome

1. Using a paring knife or cookie cutter, cut a 2-inch (5 cm) hole in the center of each bread slice. Spread the bread—including the cut-out circles—on both sides with 2 tablespoons of the room-temperature butter. (Save the remainder for the eggs.)

2. Heat your griddle or plancha to medium-high.

3. Lay the bacon strips on the griddle and cook until crisp and browned on both sides, 2 minutes per side. Set the bacon aside and keep warm.

4. Impale the cold butter on a fork and melt half of it on the griddle over the bacon fat. Place the buttered bread slices and circles on top. Cook until the bottoms start to brown, 1 minute.

5. Place a pea-sized piece of the room-temperature butter (or ½ teaspoon oil) in the center of each hole in each bread slice. When it melts, crack an egg into each hole. Season with salt and pepper. Cook the eggs and toasts until they are browned on the bottom, 2 minutes or so. If the toast starts to dry out or burn, place a couple of pea-sized pieces of room-temperature butter on the griddle at the edge. Cover with a griddle dome to speed up the cooking.

6. Slide a spatula under one of the toasts and lift it (being careful not to break the egg yolk). Butter the griddle beneath it with half the remaining room-temperature butter, then gently invert the toast and bread circle onto the butter. Repeat with the other toast. Cook until browned on the bottom and the yolks are cooked to taste, 1 to 2 minutes if you like them runny, a little longer for firmer eggs. Season with salt and pepper and add the remaining room-temperature butter or oil as needed. Again, cover with the griddle dome.

7. Transfer the toasts with their circles and the bacon to warm plates. Sprinkle with chives (if using) and dig in.

WHAT ELSE In place of the Wonder Bread of yesteryear, you now have the choice of artisanal country-style bread, multigrain, slow-fermented sourdough, and a dozen other interesting loaves.

WHAT'S MORE For a super-rich version of Bacon and Eggs in a Hole, prepare the French toast on page 39, cutting a 2-inch (5 cm) circle in the center of each slice of bread. Cook one side as directed, cracking an egg into the hole. Invert and continue cooking as directed in Step 3.

JARED'S BACON, EGG, AND DONUT BREAKFAST SANDWICH

MAKES 2 SANDWICHES (CAN BE MULTIPLIED AS DESIRED)

The world of griddles abounds with breakfast sandwiches. Jared's BED (Bacon, Egg, and Donut) takes the concept over the top. Jared Reiter is my social media manager, and since he's been onboard, we've been going viral a lot. Like 16 million views on one post and multimillion views on a dozen others. When it comes to breakfast, Jared takes an equally over-the-top approach. Like this sandwich, which starts with a donut that Jared splits and griddles. Of course, there's bacon—providing a salty yang to the donut's sweet yin. (The rendered bacon fat makes an excellent grease for the griddle.) Top that with a fried egg and maybe a side of Smash Browns (page 209), and you've got a breakfast that will keep you going all day.

Canola or olive oil for the griddle

4 strips bacon

2 tablespoons cold unsalted butter in a chunk for the griddle (or as needed)

2 donuts, cut in half through the side

2 large eggs (preferably organic)

Coarse salt (sea or kosher) and freshly ground black pepper

Maple syrup or hot sauce (or both) for drizzling

YOU'LL ALSO NEED

A griddle dome (optional)

---

1. Heat your griddle or plancha to medium-high with a cool zone over low. Lightly oil it. Arrange the bacon on the griddle and cook until crisp, 2 to 3 minutes per side. Transfer the bacon to the cool zone of the griddle.

2. Impale the butter on a fork and melt a little of it over the bacon fat. Cook the donut halves, cut side down, on the griddle until lightly browned and crisp, 1 to 2 minutes. Move the donuts to the cool zone of the griddle.

(recipe continues)

3. Melt more of the butter on the griddle to form two 5-inch (13 cm) circles. Crack the eggs onto these circles and fry for 2 to 3 minutes for sunny-side up. Season with salt and pepper. (Cover with a griddle dome to speed up the cooking.) If you prefer your eggs over easy, flip them with a spatula and cook for 1 to 2 minutes more.

4. To assemble, place the bacon slices on the bottom donut halves. Place the fried eggs on top. Drizzle with a little maple syrup and/or hot sauce and place the second donut half on top. Thanks, Jared.

WHAT ELSE There are lots of options for donuts. Jared favors apple cider donuts with cinnamon sugar. I'm partial to glazed donuts, and I prefer yeasted to cake, but either will work. I like to drizzle this sandwich with maple syrup; Jared, with hot sauce. So here's a compromise: Use equal parts maple sugar *and* hot sauce.

WHAT'S MORE You'll notice we did not include the usual slice of cheese in this recipe. Jared feels that sharp cheese and sweet donuts are just one step too far. But you can certainly add a slice of Swiss or American cheese if you desire.

LIMONCELLO PANCAKES

MAKES 40 TO 48 SILVER DOLLAR PANCAKES, SERVES 6 TO 8

For many people, the first meal they cook on a griddle is breakfast. While it's possible to cook bacon and eggs on a grill (I've done it—see my book *Project Fire*), you cannot grill a pancake. No, for that you need a griddle—ideally greased with butter or bacon fat. So what makes a great pancake? A hint of whole wheat or buckwheat flour to give the batter extra flavor. Lemon zest and limoncello (Italian lemon liqueur) for fragrance and optional poppy seeds for crunch. Finally, I like to make pancakes small, like silver dollars, to give you a higher ratio of crisp edges to soft pancake. You can always make larger pancakes if you're pressed for time. Note: If you have a large measuring cup, mix the batter in that. The spout makes it easy to pour out the right amount of batter for each pancake.

1½ cups (190 g) unbleached all-purpose flour

½ cup (75 g) whole wheat flour, buckwheat flour, or rye flour (or more all-purpose flour)

2 tablespoons granulated sugar

2 tablespoons poppy seeds (optional)

2 teaspoons baking powder

1 teaspoon baking soda

1 teaspoon coarse salt (sea or kosher)

2 teaspoons freshly and finely grated lemon zest, or to taste

1 cup (240 ml) milk (whole or skim)

1 cup (240 ml) buttermilk (or more whole or skim milk)

1 tablespoon limoncello or orange-flavored liqueur such as Cointreau

2 large eggs (preferably organic), lightly beaten with a fork

2 tablespoons melted unsalted butter (or olive oil or vegetable oil), plus 2 tablespoons cold unsalted butter in a chunk for the griddle, or bacon fat or vegetable oil (or a mixture)

1 teaspoon pure vanilla extract

Confectioners' sugar, maple syrup, jam, lemon curd, or the toppings of your choice

---

1. Place the flours, granulated sugar, poppy seeds, baking powder, baking soda, salt, and lemon zest in a large mixing bowl and whisk to mix. Make a depression in the center and add the milks, limoncello, eggs, melted butter, and vanilla. Whisk the ingredients into a fairly smooth batter, working from the center outward. Whisk just to mix; a few lumps are okay. Over-whisking will make the pancakes tough and affect their loft. Alternatively, mix the batter in a blender.

(recipe continues)

2. Meanwhile, heat your griddle or plancha to medium-high.

3. Impale the cold butter on a fork and use it to grease your griddle. Alternatively, grease the griddle with vegetable oil or bacon fat.

4. Ladle or pour the pancake batter onto the griddle to form 2-inch (5 cm) pancakes, leaving 2 inches (5 cm) between them. Cook until sizzling and browned on the bottom (watch them rise), 2 minutes, then invert and cook the other side the same way. Continue buttering the griddle between batches to keep the pancakes from sticking.

5. Transfer the pancakes to a platter or warm plates. Serve with whatever topping(s) you desire.

WHAT ELSE I suspect that thanks to your new griddle, you'll be making a lot of pancakes. Mix up a double or triple batch of the dry ingredients (minus the lemon zest) and store them in your pantry; they'll keep for several weeks. If you're serving pancakes as part of a bacon-and-egg breakfast (you should), fry the bacon first and use the bacon fat to cook the pancakes.

WHAT'S MORE

- **To make blueberry pancakes** (a classic in my New England neck of the woods), add 1 to 2 cups (145 to 290 g) of fresh or frozen blueberries to the batter. The best are the small wild blueberries from Maine.

- **To make chocolate malted pancakes,** add ¾ cup (5 ounces/145 g) chocolate chips and 3 tablespoons malt powder to the batter. (Omit the poppy seeds and lemon zest.) Okay, I admit I'm a little too old for chocolate for breakfast, but the younger members of my family can't seem to get enough.

VERY FRENCH TOAST

SERVES 2 TO 4 (CAN BE MULTIPLIED AS DESIRED)

Call it a breakfast classic. Call it the resurrection of stale bread. The French have the right idea, dubbing it pain perdu, literally "lost bread," and it reflects their primal impulse to avoid wasting food. Thanks to a soak in a milk and egg batter, the lost bread gets found—and it's about to find its way onto your griddle. So what defines great French toast? It's sizzling and crisp on the outside and creamy-soft within. Some people serve it with maple syrup; others, with a dusting of cinnamon sugar or confectioners' sugar. Gluttons like me use both.

---

4 thick slices brioche, challah, country-style white bread, or baguette (see Note)—fresh or stale

2 large eggs (preferably organic)

1 cup (240 ml) whole milk or half-and-half

1 teaspoon pure vanilla extract

Optional flavorings (any or all of the following):

    1 tablespoon orange liqueur, such as Grand Marnier, Cointreau, or triple sec

    1 teaspoon orange flower or rose water (available at Middle Eastern markets), or a combination

1 teaspoon freshly and finely grated lemon zest

½ teaspoon almond extract

2 tablespoons cold unsalted butter in a chunk, or as needed

Vegetable or extra virgin olive oil

Cinnamon sugar, confectioners' sugar, or pure maple syrup

YOU'LL ALSO NEED

A griddle dome

---

1. Arrange the bread slices in a deep baking dish just large enough to hold them. Place the eggs in a bowl and whisk until mixed. Whisk in the milk, vanilla extract, and optional flavorings. Pour this mixture over the bread slices. Soak the bread slices until soft, 5 to 10 minutes, carefully turning a couple times with a spatula so the bread soaks through evenly.

2. Meanwhile, heat your griddle or plancha to medium-high. Just before cooking, impale the butter on a fork and rub it over the griddle, covering just enough area to cook the French toast.

(recipe continues)

3. Arrange the bread slices on the griddle and cook until sizzling and browned on the bottom, 2 to 4 minutes. Invert the bread slices with a spatula, oiling the griddle with additional butter or vegetable oil to keep the French toast from sticking. Cook the other side the same way. You can place a griddle dome over the French toast to speed up the cooking.

4. Transfer the French toast to a warmed platter or plates and serve with your topping of choice.

Note: The bread slices should be ¾ inch (2 cm) thick. If using baguette, slice it sharply on the diagonal to increase the surface area of each piece.

WHAT ELSE French toast is incredibly versatile. Vanilla and almond extract are two traditional flavorings for the batter, but you can also add white wine or Marsala, or grated citrus zest. (See the Torrijas on page 238.) My daughter makes her French toast batter with equal parts half-and-half and orange juice (avoid lower fat milks, which will curdle). For bread, you can use country-style white, French bread, challah, or brioche. Some people cut pockets in the side of each bread slice and stuff them with bananas or sliced guava paste.

WHAT'S MORE One of my favorite French toasts was served at the late Grand Bay Hotel in Miami. (Why bring up a former hotel? That's where my wife and I were married!) Soak the French toast as directed in the recipe. Have ready in a baking dish 2 cups (120 g) lightly crushed cornflakes (crush them in a resealable plastic bag, using a rolling pin). Dip each slice of French toast in cornflakes on both sides, gently pressing to crust them, then griddle as directed.

You can also make savory French toast to serve as a light lunch or side dish for dinner. Soak the bread in the egg mixture, omitting the vanilla extract and optional flavorings, and adding salt, pepper, a couple of minced scallions, and freshly and finely grated lemon zest. Cook the French toast as directed in the recipe. Serve with about 1 cup (3½ ounces/100 g) freshly and finely grated Parmigiano-Reggiano sprinkled on top.

NOT YOUR USUAL HASH BROWNS

SERVES 3 OR 4

Hash browns are one of the high holies of a diner breakfast—buttery-crisp on the outside, melting within, and assertively seasoned with salt and pepper, as any proper potato dish warrants. Tradition calls for adding onion, which is delicious, but I find the earthy fragrance of leeks more interesting. Hash browns may play a supporting role to fried eggs, but breakfast would be a sorry meal without them.

1½ pounds (680 g) potatoes (preferably russets), peeled

1 leek, trimmed, washed to remove any grit, and well drained (see box), or 1 medium onion, peeled and quartered

2 to 4 tablespoons cold unsalted butter in a chunk for the griddle, or bacon fat or vegetable oil (or a mixture)

Coarse salt (sea or kosher) and freshly ground black pepper

YOU'LL ALSO NEED

A food processor fitted with a coarse shredding disk, or a box grater

A griddle press (or cast-iron skillet)

---

1. Coarsely grate the potatoes in a food processor or on a box grater. Place in a strainer and rinse under cold running water until the water runs clear, 3 minutes. Drain well. Grab handfuls of the shredded potatoes and squeeze in your hands to wring out all the excess water.

2. If using leeks, cut lengthwise into matchstick slivers and stir them into the drained potatoes. If using onion, shred in a food processor or on a box grater, wring it out with your hands, and stir it in.

3. Meanwhile, heat your griddle or plancha to medium.

4. Impale the butter on a fork and melt half of it on the griddle, or grease the griddle with bacon fat or oil. Arrange the potato mixture on the greased griddle, patting it into a slab no more than ½ inch (1 cm) thick. Season generously with salt and pepper.

5. Place a griddle press on top of the potatoes to help them brown, and cook until sizzling and darkly browned on the bottom, 5 to 8 minutes, or as needed. Slide the potatoes to another section of your griddle.

6. Grease the griddle with the remaining butter, bacon fat, or oil. Remove the griddle press and invert the hash brown slab onto the fat. Season again with salt and pepper.

Continue cooking until sizzling and browned on the bottom and the hash browns are cooked through, another 5 to 8 minutes. Add butter or oil as needed and use a griddle press to speed up the browning. Use your spatula to cut the slab into pieces, and serve hot off the griddle.

WHAT ELSE A dish that contains one primary ingredient (grated potatoes) would seem like a fail-proof recipe, but unless you use the right potato (russets or Yukon Golds) and remove all the liquid and excess starch, they just won't fry up or taste right.

WHAT'S MORE Grated sweet potatoes make wonderful hash browns. Omit the rinsing (sweet potatoes are drier than white potatoes) but wring out any excess liquid. Wring out the liquid in the onion. Cook over a lower temperature to keep from burning the plant sugars in the potatoes.

- **To make orange and white hash browns:** Use half white potatoes and half sweet potatoes. Here, you'll want to rinse the white potatoes and wring dry. Wring out the liquid in the onions.

- **To make ham hash browns:** Prepare the hash browns as directed in the recipe, adding 2 ounces (60 g) of thinly slivered smoked ham or prosciutto to the potatoes after you have wrung them dry. Use onions or leeks for these hash browns.

HOW TO TRIM AND WASH A LEEK

Cut the dark green leaves off the leeks and discard. To clean the leeks, make a lengthwise cut from the green end halfway toward the root end. Roll the leek 90 degrees and make a second lengthwise cut halfway toward the root end. (Leave the furry root end intact for the moment.) Plunge the leek, cut end down, in a bowl of cold water, moving it up and down as you would a plumber's plunger, to wash out any grit. Shake the leeks to remove the excess water, then blot dry with paper towels. Trim off and discard the furry root end and cut the leeks lengthwise into matchstick slivers.

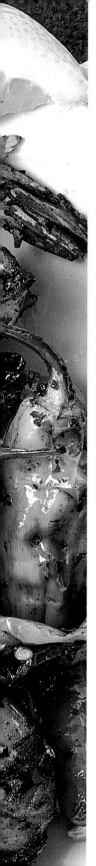

CHAPTER 2

TAPAS

Born as simple bar snacks in Spain, tapas have evolved into a dazzling array of small bite dishes that have taken over the world. The term comes from tapar, literally "to cover." Tradition has it that these small plates of big-flavor food were served atop wine glasses—either to take up less space at bar counters or to keep flies away from the wine. Hmm. A simple Spanish bar might serve six to eight tapas; a good place fifteen to twenty. In this chapter, you'll master some of Spain's most famous tapas, from bacon-seared dates to sizzling tapas bar mushrooms. Plus a Cyprus-inspired tapa and a new patatas bravas that slashes the fat found in the traditional version. Get ready for:

BACON-SEARED DATES

MAKES 16, SERVES 4

Here's a popular tapas bar snack that pits the creamy sweetness of dates against the salty tang of bacon and Cabrales blue cheese, and you come out the winner. When you cook it right, the crisp bacon gives way to the creamy dates and oozy Cabrales—a perfect contrast of textures and flavors.

---

16 pitted Medjool dates or other soft sweet dates

3 ounces (85 g) Cabrales cheese or other favorite blue cheese, cut into 16 equal slivers

5 or 6 slices of thin bacon (see What Else), gently stretched lengthwise and each cut crosswise into thirds

Extra virgin olive oil for the griddle

YOU'LL ALSO NEED
Toothpicks

---

1. Make a slit in the long side of each date. Stuff each with a sliver of Cabrales cheese. Wrap each date crosswise in bacon, securing the bacon with a toothpick.

2. Heat your griddle or plancha to medium-high and oil it well.

3. Arrange the dates on the griddle and grill until sizzling and browned on the outside and hot in the center, 2 to 3 minutes per side; 4 to 6 minutes in all.

4. Transfer the dates to paper towels to drain, then arrange on a platter or plates and serve while still sizzling hot.

WHAT ELSE Make your life easy and buy pitted dates for this recipe. Likewise, for the bacon, thin works better than thick. (Yes, I know, thin-sliced bacons tend to come from big commercial food processors, but they're easy to wrap around the dates. Better yet, use thick-sliced, real woodsmoked artisanal bacon and flatten it with a rolling pin between two sheets of parchment paper.) Cabrales is a tangy blue cheese from Asturias, Spain. If unavailable, substitute French Roquefort or Italian Gorgonzola.

WHAT'S MORE The beauty of this simple appetizer is its almost limitless variations. Stuff the dates with Marcona almonds or slivered chorizo instead of Cabrales cheese. For that matter, you could griddle the dates wrapped in thinly sliced serrano ham in place of bacon. Or substitute pitted prunes for the dates.

TAPAS BAR MUSHROOMS
WITH GARLIC PARSLEY LEMON BUTTER

MAKES 12, SERVES 3 OR 4

One small measure of Spain's tapas obsession is the Mesón del Champiñón in Madrid. Since 1964, this postage stamp–size tapas bar, tucked into the ramparts below the Plaza Real, has specialized in one specific tapa: mushrooms blasted with garlic, parsley, and lemon and sizzled on the plancha. The preparation is simple, but the results explode with flavor.

12 large white mushrooms, cleaned

1 clove garlic, peeled and minced

Coarse salt (sea or kosher) and freshly ground black pepper

8 tablespoons (1 stick/115 g) unsalted butter, at room temperature

1 cup (65 g) minced fresh flat-leaf parsley or basil, plus 12 leaves for garnish

2 tablespoons minced chives or scallion greens

½ teaspoon freshly grated lemon zest

2 teaspoons fresh lemon juice, or to taste

Olive oil for the plancha

YOU'LL ALSO NEED

A melon baller (optional)

A griddle dome

1. Using a melon baller or spoon, remove the mushroom stems to make a hollow cavity in the caps. (Save the stems for stock.)

2. Place the garlic, salt, and pepper in a mixing bowl and mash to a paste with a wooden spoon. Stir in the butter, parsley, chives, lemon zest, and lemon juice until incorporated.

3. Meanwhile, heat your griddle or plancha to medium-high in one zone and medium in another.

4. Melt 2 tablespoons of the garlic parsley butter on the medium-high zone of the griddle. Add olive oil and spread with a metal spatula. Arrange the mushroom caps hollow sides down on top and cook until the edges are browned, 2 to 3 minutes.

(recipe continues)

5. Turn the mushroom caps over and spoon garlic parsley butter into each. Move the mushrooms to the medium zone and cover with a griddle dome.

6. Continue cooking until the garlic butter is sizzling, the mushroom bottoms are browned, and the sides are soft, 4 to 6 minutes or as needed.

7. Transfer the mushrooms to a platter or plates for serving.

WHAT ELSE Look for large, clean white mushrooms (sometimes sold as stuffing mushrooms) or use baby portobellos. I call for 12 mushrooms here— that way, you can serve two, three, or four people equitably. Use a griddle dome to speed up the cooking. Note: The traditional recipe calls for flat-leaf parsley. Mrs. Raichlen does not like parsley. So at home we substitute fresh basil. The flavor is out of this world.

WHAT'S MORE Mesón del Champiñón finishes its mushrooms with crisp slivers of dry (cured) Spanish chorizo. I left it out for people who don't eat meat, but if you're so inclined (and you should be), start with 3 or 4 thin slices of hard chorizo. Cut them into matchstick slivers and crisp them in a little olive oil on the griddle or plancha. Your mushrooms will taste all the more awesome.

MANCHEGO CHEESE CRISPS

MAKES 12, SERVES 3 OR 4 (CAN BE MULTIPLIED AS DESIRED)

Here's a tapa made with two quintessentially Spanish ingredients, although I've never actually seen it at a tapas bar in Spain. It involves a cool trick (one that you might recognize—see What's More): You cook grated Manchego cheese on a plancha for just long enough to melt it, but not so long as to reduce it to an oily puddle. The resulting pancake crisps upon cooling, and when you get it right, shatters into buttery, cheesy shards when you take a bite. By way of an accent, you sprinkle it with pimentón, Spain's smoked paprika—extra points if the latter is picante (hot).

About 2 cups (8 ounces/225 g)
    coarsely grated Manchego cheese
    (rind removed before grating)
Pimentón (see What Else) for dusting

YOU'LL ALSO NEED
A wire cooling rack

1. Heat your griddle or plancha to medium. Set a wire rack over a sheet pan and set aside. Spoon out the grated cheese into 12 circles on the hot griddle each about 2 inches (5 cm) in diameter (you may need to do this in batches).

2. Cook the cheese until it is melted and the fat starts to separate out, 2 minutes. Use a thin-bladed metal spatula to turn the crisps; cook the other side the same way. Immediately transfer the cheese with the spatula to the prepared wire rack to cool. The cheese will crisp on cooling. Dust the top with pimentón before serving.

WHAT ELSE Manchego is a sheep's milk cheese from Spain's La Mancha region—available aged 40 days up to 2 years—the older, the richer the flavor. Once available only in specialty shops, Manchego can now be found at most supermarkets. One good brand of pimentón picante is La Chinata—available online. Alternatively, substitute hot paprika or ground cayenne.

WHAT'S MORE If this preparation sounds familiar, you've probably experienced frico, an Italian cheese crisp made with grated Parmigiano-Reggiano. (Either that, or you watch a lot of Instagram reels.) I've made cheese crisps with every grate-able cheese from cheddar to pecorino. You can also make a large disk and fold it in half while still warm to form a taco shell (stand it in a taco mold until cool).

GRIDDLED FIGS AND HALLOUMI CHEESE

SERVES 4

Sweet figs and salty cheese are an ancient Mediterranean flavor combination that is as compelling today as it was in the time of Homer. A hot griddle puts a crust on the cheese and gives the figs a sugary crunch. This is one of those singular dishes that works equally well as an appetizer or as a dessert.

Extra virgin olive oil for oiling and brushing

1 pound (455 g) Halloumi cheese, cut into ½-inch-thick (1 cm) slabs

6 to 8 ripe fresh figs, stemmed and halved from top to bottom

¾ cup (150 g) sugar in a small shallow dish

Honey or saba (grape must syrup) for drizzling

¼ cup (35 g) toasted pine nuts or slivered almonds (see box)

1. Heat your griddle or plancha to medium-high. Oil it well with olive oil.

2. Meanwhile, lightly brush the Halloumi on both sides with olive oil. Arrange on the griddle and cook until sizzling and browned on both sides, 2 to 4 minutes per side, turning with a spatula.

HOW TO TOAST PINE NUTS, ALMONDS, AND OTHER NUTS

Place the nuts in a dry skillet and roast over medium-high heat until fragrant and lightly browned, 5 minutes, shaking the pan or stirring the nuts with a wooden spoon, so they toast evenly. Immediately, transfer the nuts to a bowl to cool. Note: You can also toast the nuts on the plancha. In this case, use an offset spatula to corral and turn them.

(recipe continues)

3. Brush the cut part of the figs with olive oil. Dip the cut side of each fig half in sugar, shaking off the excess. Arrange sugar side down on the griddle and cook until sizzling and browned, 2 to 4 minutes.

4. To serve, arrange the hot cheese on a platter or plates. Arrange the figs, caramelized side up, on top. Drizzle with honey and sprinkle with pine nuts.

WHAT ELSE Halloumi is a firm, salty cheese made from goat, sheep, and/or cows' milk on the island of Cyprus. It has the genial property of browning without melting when seared on a hot griddle or plancha. Look for it at cheese shops and most supermarkets.

WHAT'S MORE Can't find Halloumi? Use Greek cheeses like graviera, kefalotyri, and kefalograviera, or even fresh mozzarella. (If using the last, lightly dust each slice with flour before griddling.) Can't find fresh figs? Use peach or nectarine quarters or plum halves. Sometimes I drizzle the fruit and cheese with balsamic syrup or pomegranate molasses instead of honey.

FIRE CRACKERS

(GRIDDLED SALTINES WITH HOT PAPRIKA AND GOAT CHEESE–FILLED PIQUILLOS)

MAKES 12, SERVES 2 TO 4

I first tasted fire crackers at a restaurant in California's Santa Ynez Valley; here they get the tapas bar treatment with Spanish olive oil and pimentón picante (spicy smoked paprika)—and by crisping on the plancha. By way of a topping, I suggest another popular Spanish tapa: piquillo peppers stuffed with goat cheese. Piquillos are small, sweet-smoky, fire-roasted red peppers almost always sold in jars. Look for them at specialty shops or online.

FOR THE FIRE CRACKERS

2 tablespoons unsalted butter

2 tablespoons extra virgin olive oil, plus more for the griddle

1 teaspoon of your favorite hot sauce (I like Crystal; optional)

12 saltine crackers (or wheat crackers of your choice)

Freshly ground black pepper

La Chinata pimentón picante (see What Else)

FOR THE TOPPING

12 piquillo peppers, drained

6 tablespoons (45 g) soft creamy goat cheese, like Montrachet

YOU'LL ALSO NEED

A pastry brush

A wire cooling rack

1. Melt the butter in a small pan and add the 2 tablespoons olive oil and the hot sauce (if using). Let cool almost to room temperature. Using a pastry brush, brush the saltines on both sides with this mixture. Season heavily on both sides with black pepper and the pimentón picante.

2. Heat your griddle or plancha to medium-high. Lightly oil with olive oil.

3. Arrange the crackers on the griddle and cook until lightly toasted on both sides, 1 to 2 minutes per side. Light browning is okay, but don't let the crackers burn.

4. Transfer the crackers to a wire rack to cool to room temperature (they'll crisp on cooling).

5. While the crackers cool, stuff the piquillo peppers with goat cheese. (Use two spoons or a piping bag.)

6. Place a cheese-stuffed pepper on each cracker and dig in.

WHAT ELSE The fire in these crackers comes from La Chinata picante— a flaked smoked hot pepper from the La Vera region in Caceres, Spain. You can order it online or substitute regular pimentón (smoked paprika) or sweet paprika plus a shake of ground cayenne.

WHAT'S MORE I call for saltine crackers here, but you can certainly make these with your favorite upscale crackers, such as Carr's. For that matter, toast points made from thinly sliced baguette or country-style white bread are pretty awesome, too.

For Cajun fire crackers, substitute blackening spice for the pimentón. For a Maryland version, use Old Bay seasoning instead.

A NEW PATATAS BRAVAS

SERVES 4

Ten years ago, few Americans had ever heard of patatas bravas ("brave" or "angry" potatoes in Spanish). Today, these crusty potatoes dipped in or doused with spicy tomato sauce turn up at restaurants not just across Spain, but across the US and around the world. Tradition calls for deep-frying the potatoes, which makes them crisp but heavy. The technique that follows was developed by Michelin-starred chef and fellow Windstar cruise ship consultant Anthony Sasso, who smashes the potatoes on a sizzling plancha, delivering all the potato crispness with a fraction of the fat. The results are some of the most satisfying patatas bravas I've had in ages. Note: Here in Miami, patatas bravas are often called papas bravas. So what makes them brava (angry)? A spicy tomato sauce fired with serrano and guindilla chiles.

1½ pounds (680 g) fingerling or baby potatoes (or larger potatoes cut into 1 by 2-inch/3 by 5 cm pieces)

Coarse salt (sea or kosher)

2 tablespoons extra virgin olive oil, plus more for the griddle

1 pickled or dried guindilla chile, sliced paper-thin crosswise (optional)

1 serrano chile, seeded and minced (for a spicier sauce, leave the seeds in)

1 small onion, peeled and finely chopped

1 clove garlic, peeled and minced

2 teaspoons pimentón (smoked paprika)

1 to 2 teaspoons hot paprika or ¼ teaspoon ground cayenne pepper

1 can (14.5 ounces/411 g) diced fire-roasted tomatoes (one good brand is Muir Glen Organic)

1 tablespoon Spanish sherry vinegar or red wine vinegar

1 teaspoon sugar

Freshly ground black pepper

YOU'LL ALSO NEED

A griddle press (or cast-iron skillet)

---

1. Scrub the potatoes clean with a stiff-bristled brush. Place in a large saucepan with cold salted water to cover. Bring to a boil, reduce the heat, and simmer the potatoes until soft, 10 to 12 minutes. (Pierce with a knife or skewer to assess doneness.) Drain in a colander, rinse with cold water, and drain well again. The potatoes can be boiled up to 24 hours ahead and refrigerated until ready to use.

(recipe continues)

2. Make the salsa brava: Heat the oil in a saucepan over medium heat. Add the guindilla (if using), serrano, onion, and garlic to the saucepan and fry until golden brown, 3 to 5 minutes, stirring with a wooden spoon. Add the pimentón and hot paprika or cayenne and cook for 1 minute. Add the tomatoes, vinegar, and sugar.

3. Gently simmer the sauce until richly flavored, 5 to 8 minutes. Puree with an immersion blender or in a conventional blender. Correct the seasoning, adding salt, pepper, or cayenne to taste: The sauce should be highly seasoned. The sauce can be prepared several hours ahead to this stage.

4. Just before serving, heat your griddle or plancha to medium-high. Oil it well with olive oil. Blot the potatoes dry. Arrange them on the plancha and cook until sizzling, 2 minutes. Smash them with a griddle press—enough to break the skin and flatten them, but not so much that you pulverize the potatoes. Continue griddling until the potatoes are hot and crisp, turning once or twice, 2 to 4 minutes more per side.

5. Transfer the potatoes to a platter or plates and sprinkle with salt. Spoon the salsa brava over them, or serve it in ramekins next to the potatoes for dipping.

WHAT ELSE For the best results, use a fingerling (small) potato, like Baby Dutch Yellow. Parboiling the potatoes makes them easier for smashing. You can also roast them until soft on the griddle (use a griddle dome). Guindilla chiles give the sauce its kick. They are long, slender medium-hot Spanish peppers—usually sold pickled in brine or dried. Look for them in Spanish markets or substitute a diced serrano or jalapeño chile, either of which will give you the requisite heat.

WHAT'S MORE Once you master the basic technique of smashing and griddling potatoes, you can use it for a wide variety of vegetables, from parsnips to Jerusalem artichokes. Salsa brava makes a great dipping sauce for griddled asparagus or broccoli.

TAPAS BAR SHRIMP
(GRILLED SHRIMP WITH PEPPERS)

SERVES 4 AS AN APPETIZER, 2 OR 3 AS A MAIN COURSE

This dish combines two classic Spanish tapas. The first is camarones al ajillo, garlic shrimp sizzled in olive oil in a shallow earthenware dish known as a cazuela. The second—fire-blistered padrón peppers—are devoured by the plateful with your fingers. I've brought them together, harnessing the flavor-boosting powers of a hot griddle.

---

1 pound (455 g) extra-large shrimp (U-15s), shelled and deveined

6 ounces (170 g) padrón or shishito peppers

1 tablespoon extra virgin olive oil (preferably Spanish), plus 2 to 3 tablespoons for the griddle

2 cloves garlic, peeled and crushed with the side of a knife

3 tablespoons minced fresh flat-leaf parsley

1 teaspoon smoked or sweet paprika

½ to 1 teaspoon hot red pepper flakes

Coarse salt (sea or kosher) and freshly ground black pepper

2 to 3 tablespoons sherry or brandy (optional)

Lemon wedges, for serving

YOU'LL ALSO NEED

A long-handled match or butane match (optional)

---

1. Place the shrimp and peppers in a mixing bowl with 1 tablespoon of the olive oil, the garlic, 2 tablespoons of the parsley, smoked paprika, hot red pepper flakes, and salt and pepper. Toss to mix and coat the shrimp. Let marinate while you heat the plancha.

2. Heat your griddle or plancha to high. Drizzle it with 2 tablespoons of olive oil and spread the oil around with a spatula.

(recipe continues)

Tapas 59

3. Spoon the shrimp and peppers onto the hot plancha. Cook until the shrimp are browned on the bottom, 1 to 2 minutes. Turn the shrimp and peppers with the spatula and continue cooking until the other side are browned, 1 to 2 minutes.

4. If using the sherry or brandy, pour it over the shrimp and cook until evaporated. For high drama, if using brandy, touch a lit long fireplace match or butane match to it to flambé it.

5. Transfer the shrimp and peppers to a platter or plates and sprinkle with the remaining 1 tablespoon parsley. Serve with lemon wedges for squeezing.

WHAT ELSE I call for hot pepper flakes here, but in Spain, you'd use a dried hot chile known as guindilla (which is sliced crosswise into paper-thin circles). Hot red pepper flakes make a fine substitute. If you can find head-on shrimp, this dish will taste all that much better. If you can't find padrón peppers, use their Japanese cousins, shishitos. Both are available at most supermarkets. Finally, I've made the sherry optional. It adds a sweet, nutty finish, but I'd hate to ask you buy a whole bottle just to use a couple tablespoons.

WHAT'S MORE This preparation lends itself to all manner of seafood, from scallops to squid to tiny cuttlefish known in Spain as chipirones. For an American Southwestern twist, substitute slivered poblano chiles for the padróns and chili powder for the smoked paprika.

Griddle Feast

A TAPAS COCKTAIL PARTY

Tapas is the name given to traditional Spanish bar snacks—a dish of marinated olives, for example, or spicy sliced chorizo or shrimp sizzled with olive oil and garlic. Over the years, tapas have evolved into a stunning array of small-format dishes not just in Spain but the world over. Tapas are traditionally enjoyed with wine, sherry, vermouth, or sangria in the innumerable bars that dot Spain (more than 40,000). Sounds to me like the perfect fare for a cocktail party—wherever you reside and whatever you're drinking. Note: For here and the other Griddle Feasts, heat your griddle to the temperature designated in the individual recipes, with one zone on low for keeping the various items warm.

Here's what's on the menu:

- Manchego Cheese Crisps (page 50)
- Fire Crackers (Griddled Saltines with Hot Paprika and Goat Cheese–Filled Piquillos) (page 54)
- Bacon-Seared Dates (page 46)
- Tapas Bar Mushrooms with Garlic Parsley Lemon Butter (page 47)
- A New Patatas Bravas (page 56)
- Tapas Bar Shrimp (Grilled Shrimp with Peppers) (page 59)

Here's how to sequence the preparation:

The night before:
- Boil the potatoes for the patatas bravas.

Before the meal prep:
- Stuff the piquillos with goat cheese for the fire crackers.
- Make the Manchego cheese crisps. Let cool and serve.

The actual cook (serve each dish sequentially as it comes off the griddle):
- Heat your griddle or plancha with one zone on medium-high, one on medium, and one on low for warming. Oil the griddle.
- Start by griddling the crackers for the fire crackers on the medium-high zone. Assemble and serve the fire crackers.
- Prepare the bacon-seared dates and cook on the medium-high zone. Reserve the rendered bacon fat for the patatas bravas.
- Prepare the patatas bravas and cook on the medium-high zone.
- Prepare the tapas bar mushrooms. Cook the mushrooms on the medium-high and medium zones.
- Turn one zone up to high. Prepare the tapas bar shrimp and cook on the high zone.

CHAPTER 3

SANDWICHES

Think of the world's great sandwiches. The Cuban medianoche. The New Orleans muffuletta. And of course, the Philadelphia cheesesteak. All start their path to gustatory greatness on a griddle. This chapter introduces the essential divide-and-conquer method. Used together with the griddle dome, this technique enables you to cook thick sandwiches in halves, uniting them when each ingredient is at its sizzling best.

BLT AND COMPANY

MAKES 2 SANDWICHES (CAN BE MULTIPLIED AS DESIRED)

The BLT may be the most perfect sandwich ever invented—perfect in its contrast of colors, textures, temperatures, and tastes. After all, how many sandwiches run hot and cold? Soft and crisp? Salty, smoky, and fruity? (Don't forget: Tomato is actually a fruit.) It used to be that to make a BLT at home, you needed a toaster and a frying pan (which is probably why most people eat their BLTs at the local diner). The griddle makes for one-stop cooking. Note: I like to serve my BLT open face—for a higher ratio of bacon, lettuce, and tomato to bread—but the conventional two slices make an awesome sandwich, too.

---

8 strips bacon

2 or 4 slices of your favorite sandwich bread (2 slices for open-face sandwiches; 4 slices for conventional)

Unsalted butter or canola or olive oil for the griddle (optional)

3 tablespoons mayonnaise (I'm partial to Hellmann's, but use your favorite)

1 juicy ripe red tomato, sliced (see What Else)

4 Boston lettuce leaves

---

1. Heat your griddle or plancha to medium-high.

2. Arrange the bacon strips on the griddle (no need to oil it first—the bacon fat will take care of that). Fry the bacon until crispy and browned on both sides, 2 to 4 minutes per side. Transfer the bacon to a paper towel to drain.

3. While the bacon cooks, scrape some of the fat to a different section of the griddle. Toast the bread in the bacon fat on the griddle, 2 to 4 minutes per side. Add butter or oil as needed, so the bread crisps.

4. Transfer the bread to a clean cotton dish cloth (the cloth will keep it from getting soggy). Generously slather it on one side with mayonnaise. Arrange the bacon strips on top, followed by the tomato and lettuce. (This is for an open-face sandwich—place the second piece of toast on top if making a conventional sandwich.)

5. Eat while the bacon is still hot and the tomato and lettuce are still cool.

WHAT ELSE There are lots of options for bacon: thick-sliced, thin-sliced, "uncured" (i.e., nitrite-free, although I've never understood why someone would want to avoid a curing salt that occurs naturally in vegetables like celery). You could even use a pastrami bacon, like the one made by yours truly in partnership with Pederson's Farms. What matters most is that you use a real smokehouse bacon (a lot of supermarket bacon acquires its taste by injecting smoke flavoring). And that you fry the bacon fresh on the griddle and assemble the sandwich hot. About the requisite T: Remember that this sandwich lives and dies by the lusciousness of its tomato. Pick the best you can find.

WHAT'S MORE A sandwich this classic invites improvisations. Of course there's the BLAT (bacon, lettuce, avocado, tomato). Here are two lesser-known variations on the theme (open-face or conventional—your call).

- **Italian BLT:** Prepare the sandwich as directed, substituting sliced or split focaccia for the bread; pancetta (Italian cured pork belly) for the bacon; and arugula for the lettuce. Alternatively (or in addition to the pancetta), use the Prosciutto Bacon on page 26.

- **Hungarian BLT:** Solina shutesh is one of the glories of Hungarian barbecue— paprika-crusted slab bacon hedge-hogged (i.e., scored in a crosshatch pattern) and roasted over a wood fire. As the bacon cooks, you carve it onto thick slices of rye bread carpeted with thinly sliced vegetables. The hot dripping bacon fat makes the sandwich that much better. Here's the *Project Griddle* version: Sprinkle the bacon slices on both sides with sweet or hot paprika. Fry the bacon and toast the bread (rye, please) as directed. Arrange the bacon slices on the bread and top with sliced onion, radishes, cucumbers, and tomatoes.

GRILLED CHEESE AND THEN SOME

MAKES 2 SANDWICHES (CAN BE MULTIPLIED AS DESIRED)

Ah, the grilled cheese sandwich. Staple of my childhood, made by my ballet dancer mother, who had little time and even less inclination for cooking. Frances Raichlen's version consisted of a slice of Velveeta cheese sandwiched between two slices of Wonder Bread, the whole pan-fried in margarine. (Okay—it tasted better then than it sounds now.) But start with a pedigreed cheese, artisanal bread, and some creative condiments, and you get a grilled cheese sandwich worth firing up your griddle for. What follows is a general methodology: Customize it as you desire.

---

4 slices of your favorite sandwich bread

2 tablespoons unsalted butter at room temperature, plus 2 tablespoons cold unsalted butter in a chunk for the griddle

1 to 2 tablespoons mustard such as Meaux-style, Dijon, Düsseldorf, or horseradish (optional)

3 tablespoons mayonnaise (preferably Hellmann's, optional)

5 to 6 ounces (145 to 170 g) cave-aged Gruyère or other meltable cheese, thinly sliced or coarsely grated (see What Else)

YOU'LL ALSO NEED
Parchment paper
A griddle dome (optional)

---

1. Butter each slice of bread on one side with the room-temperature butter. Place the bread, buttered side down, on a parchment-lined sheet pan. Slather the unbuttered side with mustard and mayonnaise (if using). Pile half of the cheese on one of the bread slices, spreading it out evenly, then place a second slice of bread, butter side up, on top; repeat with the remaining cheese and bread.

2. Meanwhile, heat your griddle or plancha to medium-high. Impale the chunk of butter on a fork and rub the butter over a section of the griddle just large enough to accommodate the sandwiches.

3. Place the sandwiches on the griddle and cook until the bottoms are sizzling and browned and the cheese starts to melt, 2 to 3 minutes. To speed up the process, cover with a griddle dome. Using an offset spatula, invert the sandwiches, re-buttering the griddle as needed. Continue cooking until the sandwiches are sizzling and browned on both sides, 4 to 6 minutes in all. Serve at once.

WHAT ELSE I make my grilled cheese sandwiches with tangy cave-aged Gruyère, with a sharp smear of mustard to counterpoint the richness. Other good candidates include sharp cheddar, Dutch Edam or Gouda, Colby cheese, pepper Jack, and so on. For even melting, coarsely grate the cheese before adding it to the sandwich. Of course, this adds a step and a piece of cookware, so I usually go the sliced cheese route.

WHAT'S MORE The grilled cheese sandwich lends itself to almost infinite variations.

- **For a Spanish-style grilled cheese,** use grated Manchego cheese. Omit the mustard and sprinkle the mayonnaise with pimentón (smoked paprika). Add drained piquillo peppers or the padrón peppers on page 59.

- **For a Mexican-style grilled cheese sandwich,** use bolillos (Mexican sandwich buns) and Oaxaca or Chihuahua cheese (or Jack or pepper Jack). Omit the mustard and sprinkle the mayonnaise with Tajín (a Mexican chile-lime seasoning powder). Add roasted poblano chile strips and sliced fresh tomato.

- **For an Alpine-style sandwich,** use Emmenthaler or raclette and drizzle with a few drops of kirsch (cherry brandy). Add thinly sliced cornichon pickles and a few slices of Swiss Bündnerfleisch or Italian bresaola (both sorts of beef "prosciutto") or the Prosciutto Bacon on page 26.

- **For a German-style sandwich,** use pumpernickel bread and Muenster or Limburger cheese and add ham. The mustard should be Düsseldorf; the ham should be Black Forest.

- **For an Italian-style sandwich,** use focaccia or ciabatta and Taleggio or fresh mozzarella. Add a few slices of mortadella.

- **For a Vermont-style grilled cheese sandwich,** use country-style white or sourdough bread and sharp cheddar cheese. Add Harrington's or other Vermont-style smoked ham and apple or cranberry chutney.

A NEW CROQUE MONSIEUR

MAKES 2 SANDWICHES (CAN BE MULTIPLIED AS DESIRED)

Start with a grilled cheese sandwich and give it a French twist. As in tangy alpine cheese. And a slice of smoky ham. Béchamel sauce. And butter—lots of butter. The result is croque monsieur—the classic sandwich served at cafés across France. Traditionally, croque monsieur would be cooked under a broiler, but it doesn't take much rejiggering to adapt it to the griddle. The secret—heretical as it sounds—is to place the béchamel sauce *inside* the sandwich, not on top. You get the same buttery crust, melty cheese, and meaty ham. Note: For a quick, if unconventional croque monsieur, replace the béchamel sauce with mayonnaise (you'll need 2 tablespoons per sandwich).

---

3 tablespoons salted butter, at room temperature, plus 2 tablespoons cold unsalted butter in a chunk for the griddle

4 slices country-style white bread (the French would probably cut the crusts off—I don't bother)

½ cup (120 ml) Béchamel Sauce (recipe follows)

4 ounces (115 g) thinly sliced smoked cooked ham (see What Else)

4 ounces (115 g) thinly sliced Gruyère cheese

YOU'LL ALSO NEED
A griddle dome

---

1. Butter all 4 slices of bread on one side and place them butter side down on a rimmed sheet pan. Slather the other side of each piece of bread with Béchamel Sauce. Lay sliced ham on top of 2 of the slices, followed by the Gruyère. Top with the remaining bread slices, butter side up.

2. Meanwhile, heat your griddle or plancha to medium. Impale the chunk of butter on a fork and butter an area of the griddle just large enough to hold the sandwiches.

3. Place the sandwiches on the griddle and top with a griddle dome. Cook until the sandwiches are sizzling and browned on both sides and the cheese in the center is melted, 3 to 6 minutes per side. Use an offset spatula—and a lot of care—to turn them. And that, *mes amis*, is how this American makes a croque monsieur.

(recipe continues)

WHAT ELSE This simple sandwich is all about the quality of its ingredients. To start, you need a dense country-style white bread, known in France as pain de mie, and sometimes called a Pullman loaf stateside. For an unconventional twist, use brioche. The ham should be smoked. (The French favor boiled or baked ham, but smoked delivers more flavor.) Hint—if it comes in perfectly square or round slices, it's a pressed ham product, not real ham. Another hint: The cheese should be Gruyère—preferably cave-aged, which has an intensity of flavor presliced "Swiss" cheese can only dream of.

BÉCHAMEL SAUCE

MAKES ½ CUP (120 ML)

Béchamel sauce is one of the defining flavors and textures of croque monsieur. Here's how you make it.

---

1 tablespoon unsalted butter

1 tablespoon all-purpose flour

½ cup (120 ml) whole milk or half-and-half

Coarse salt (sea or kosher) and freshly ground black pepper

Freshly grated nutmeg

Melt the butter in a small saucepan over medium-high heat. Whisk in the flour and cook until sizzling but not brown, 1 minute. Off the heat, whisk in the milk in a thin stream. Return the mixture to the heat and bring to a boil over medium-high heat for 2 minutes, whisking steadily. The sauce will thicken. Add salt, pepper, and nutmeg to taste. Let the béchamel sauce cool to room temperature before spreading on the bread.

THE MIDNIGHTER
(CUBAN HAM, CHEESE, PORK, AND PICKLE SANDWICH)

MAKES 2 SANDWICHES (CAN BE MULTIPLIED AS DESIRED)

Born in Cuba and perfected in Miami, the medianoche ("midnighter," literally) sandwich was the traditional post-movie snack in Havana. (Hence its name.) Today, you find it not just in Miami but across North America. The medianoche has something for everyone: salty ham, roast pork, nutty cheese, tart pickles, and sharp mustard—all packed into a sweet roll best approximated in the US by a brioche hotdog bun.

2 elongated brioche rolls or brioche hotdog rolls

2 tablespoons mayonnaise (preferably Hellmann's)

2 tablespoons Dijon mustard

4 ounces (115 g) thinly sliced Gruyère cheese

3 ounces (85 g) thinly sliced smoked ham

12 dill pickle slices

3 ounces (85 g) thinly sliced roast pork (or roast turkey or more ham)

Canola or olive oil for the griddle

2 tablespoons cold unsalted butter in a chunk for the griddle

YOU'LL ALSO NEED
Parchment paper
A griddle press (or cast-iron skillet)

1. Open the rolls like a book. Spread one side of the inside with mayonnaise; the other side with mustard. Place the cheese and ham on one side in that order, and the pickle slices and pork on the other. Place a sheet of parchment paper just large enough to cover the sandwich on top (this will keep the filling from sticking to the griddle).

2. Meanwhile, heat your griddle or plancha to medium-high. Oil an area just large enough to hold the sandwiches.

(recipe continues)

3. Carefully place the open sandwiches, parchment paper side down, on the griddle. Cover with a griddle dome and cook until the meat is sizzling and the cheese is melted, 2 to 4 minutes, or as needed.

4. Impale the butter on a fork and rub the butter on the griddle. Invert the sandwiches and peel off and discard the parchment paper. Put the top and bottom of the sandwich together (that is, close the "book").

5. Place a griddle press on top of the closed sandwiches to flatten them slightly and griddle until sizzling and browned on the bottom, 2 to 4 minutes. Turn the sandwiches with an offset spatula, and repeat on the other side. Take care that the bread (which is slightly sweet) doesn't burn.

6. Cut each sandwich in half and serve at once.

WHAT ELSE To cook the medianoche through and melt the cheese without burning the bread, work over medium heat. Place a griddle press on top of the sandwiches to give them their trademark pressed look. Don't be deterred if you don't have homemade roast pork on hand. Boar's Head makes a version you can find at the deli section of most supermarkets. Alternatively, use roast turkey breast or double up on the ham.

WHAT'S MORE For an Italian touch, use sliced porchetta in place of the smoked ham.

MUFFULETTA
(HOT NEW ORLEANS COLD CUT SANDWICH)

MAKES 2 SANDWICHES (CAN BE MULTIPLIED AS DESIRED)

It's hard to improve on a hoagie, that Philadelphian sandwich consisting of a crusty roll piled high with cold cuts and piqued with pickled hot peppers. Just don't tell that to New Orleans sandwich makers who, using similar ingredients, have created a dramatically different sandwich: the muffuletta. (The name comes from muffe, Italian slang for "a mushroom," or perhaps muffola, "mitten"—a reference to the round shape of the bread.) Start with coppa (spicy shoulder ham), sopressata (wine-cured salami), and salty prosciutto. Add sharp provolone cheese and a tangy relish of olives, oregano, and celery. Finally, and here comes the stroke of genius, serve the sandwich hot.

---

2 kaiser rolls

2 tablespoons extra virgin olive oil, plus more for the griddle

4 ounces (115 g) thinly sliced sharp provolone cheese

2 ounces (60 g) thinly sliced coppa (Italian shoulder ham)

½ cup (65 g) Olive Relish (page 80), plus more for serving

2 ounces (60 g) thinly sliced prosciutto or smoked ham

2 ounces (60 g) thinly sliced sopressata or other Italian salami

YOU'LL ALSO NEED
Parchment paper

---

1. Slice the kaiser rolls in half through the side. Brush the outsides of the rolls with 1 tablespoon of olive oil and the insides with the remainder. Place the open rolls on your work surface, cut sides up.

2. On the two bottom halves, arrange the provolone and coppa in that order. Make sure the coppa completely covers the cheese. Top each half with a piece of parchment paper.

(recipe continues)

3. On the two top halves, spread out the Olive Relish, then arrange the prosciutto and sopressata in that order on top. Top each half with a piece of parchment paper just large enough to cover the sandwich.

4. Meanwhile, heat your griddle or plancha to medium. Oil it well.

5. Carefully place the bottom sandwich halves on the griddle, meat side down (see picture below). Place the top halves meat side down, with the parchment, as

well. Cook until the meat on the bottom is sizzling and browned, 2 to 3 minutes.

6. Using an offset spatula, turn the halves over. Peel off and discard the parchment paper. Assemble the halves into two sandwiches. Cook until the outside of the rolls are toasted and browned on both sides, 2 to 4 minutes per side, turning with the spatula.

7. Cut the muffulettas in half and serve at once with any extra Olive Relish on the side.

WHAT ELSE In order to cook the muffuletta through without burning the exterior, New Orleans sandwich makers divide and conquer, cooking the top and bottom half of the sandwich separately, then putting them together. Makes sense to me.

OLIVE RELISH

MAKES ABOUT 1½ CUPS (195 G)

This tangy relish—tart with capers and salty with olives—is what makes a muffuletta a muffuletta. I call for making more than you need for two sandwiches—you'll be glad you have leftovers.

½ cup (75 g) drained pitted black olives or kalamata olives

½ cup (65 g) pimento-stuffed green olives

1 tablespoon brined capers, drained

1 celery stalk, roughly chopped

1 clove garlic, peeled and roughly chopped

3 tablespoons finely chopped fresh flat-leaf parsley

1 pickled hot pepper, roughly chopped, or ½ teaspoon hot red pepper flakes

½ teaspoon dried oregano

3 tablespoons extra virgin olive oil

1 tablespoon red wine vinegar, or to taste

Freshly ground black pepper to taste

YOU'LL ALSO NEED

A food processor

Place the black and green olives, capers, celery, garlic, parsley, pickled hot pepper or red pepper flakes, and oregano in a food processor. Coarsely chop, running the machine in short bursts. (Do not puree.) Add the olive oil, vinegar, and black pepper, and pulse the machine just to mix. Correct the seasoning, adding more vinegar and/or black pepper to taste. In the unlikely event you have any left over, store in the refrigerator: The relish will keep for at least a week.

WHAT'S MORE To make a Quick Olive Relish, combine 1 cup (160 g) drained giardiniera (Italian-style pickled vegetables), 1 cup (150 g) drained pitted black or green olives, 2 teaspoons drained capers, and 2 to 3 tablespoons extra virgin olive oil in a food processor. Coarsely chop until chunky (but not pureed). Makes 1½ cups (195 g).

CHEESESTEAKS NORTH AND SOUTH

MAKES 2 SANDWICHES (CAN BE MULTIPLIED AS DESIRED)

The cheesesteak is a Philadelphia institution—invented in the 1930s, so the story goes, by two brothers and hotdog vendors, Pat Olivieri and Harry Olivieri. Looking to beef up their repertoire (pardon the pun), the pair sizzled thinly sliced steak and onions on a griddle, piling them on a hoagie roll. The cheese (provolone) came later, as did the landmark restaurant—Pat's King of Steaks, which still supplies Philadelphia with righteous cheesesteaks today. Yes, at some sandwich shops, the "cheese" now comes from a can or tub, and mushrooms and bell peppers have become acceptable garnishes. Here's the real McCoy, plus a Southern version featuring homemade pimento cheese.

THE ESSENTIALS

8 ounces (225 g) rib eye steaks, sirloin, or top or bottom round

4 ounces (115 g) thinly sliced provolone cheese (preferably Italian and aged)

Canola or olive oil for the griddle

THE OPTIONALS

1 small sweet onion, peeled and thinly sliced

1 poblano chile or ½ green bell pepper, stemmed, seeded, and cut into ¼-inch (6 mm) strips

About 1½ cups (6 ounces/170 g) cleaned, stemmed, and thinly sliced button mushrooms

TO FINISH THE CHEESESTEAKS

2 hoagie rolls, cut almost in half through the side

Mayonnaise (preferably Hellmann's)

Chopped pickled hot peppers or hot pepper relish (optional)

YOU'LL ALSO NEED

A food processor (optional)

A griddle dome

1. Slice the steaks across the grain as thinly as possible. If using rib eye or sirloin, you can use a knife. If using top or bottom round, it helps to partially freeze the meat until it's firm, then slice it on a meat slicer or on the slicing disk of a food processor.

(recipe continues)

2. Heat your griddle or plancha with two zones, one medium-hot for cooking and one low for warming. Oil it well.

3. If using onion, peppers, and/or mushrooms: Cook the onions on the medium-high zone until browned, 2 to 4 minutes, turning with an offset spatula. Move to the low zone to keep warm. Cook the peppers and mushrooms separately the same way, then move to the low zone.

4. Re-oil the griddle. Add the steaks to the medium-high zone and cook until sizzling, browned, and cooked through, 3 to 4 minutes or to taste. (Tradition calls for the steaks to be well done.)

When the steaks are almost cooked, lay the cheese slices on top to melt. Cover with a griddle dome to speed up melting.

5. Meanwhile, warm the hoagie rolls, cut side down, on the low zone.

6. To assemble the cheesesteaks, slather the inside of the rolls with mayonnaise and top with the hot peppers, if using. Use an offset spatula to add the steaks with the melted cheese, then add the onions, peppers, and mushrooms if using. Close up the cheesesteaks and cut each in half. Get ready to sink your teeth into one of America's great sandwiches.

WHAT ELSE Most Philly cheesesteak joints use inexpensive cuts of beef, like top or bottom round, slicing it paper-thin on a meat slicer to make it tender. I like to go uptown, using thinly sliced rib eyes or sirloin. For cheese, you want provolone—imported and aged, if possible.

WHAT'S MORE As you've probably figured by now, I'm not a partisan of Cheez Whiz, but there is a creamy cheese preparation from the South that goes brilliantly on a cheesesteak: pimento cheese. To make it, you mix freshly grated sharp cheddar with cream cheese, pimientos (roasted red peppers), Tabasco sauce, and mayonnaise. If using, simply dollop a couple tablespoons over the cooked steak instead of laying down the cheese slices. See the following page— and don't tell Pat and Harry.

PIMENTO CHEESE

MAKES 2 CUPS (450 G)

This makes more than you need for two cheesesteaks, but the stuff is so good, you'll want to have extra around. Store any excess, covered, in the refrigerator—it will keep for several days.

1 jar (4 ounces/115 g) pimientos (roasted red peppers), drained

About 2 cups (8 ounces/225 g) coarsely grated sharp cheddar cheese

4 ounces (115 g) cream cheese, at room temperature

¼ cup (55 g) mayonnaise (preferably Hellmann's)

1 tablespoon Dijon mustard

1 teaspoon Tabasco sauce or other favorite hot sauce, or to taste

1 teaspoon smoked or sweet paprika

Coarse salt (sea or kosher) and freshly ground black pepper to taste

Place the ingredients in a food processor and puree to a coarse paste. Correct the seasoning, adding hot sauce and salt (if needed). The pimento cheese should be highly seasoned.

POLPETTI PO' BOY
(THE SMASHED MEATBALL SUB)

MAKES 4 SANDWICHES

The meatball sub is an Italian American icon. As luscious as the traditional version is, a griddle can help you make it even better. How? In a single word: texture. In two words: texture and taste. Meatballs simmered in tomato sauce are good. Meatballs cooked like smash burgers are better, offering crust and crunch, plus the rich Maillard flavors that come from searing and caramelizing protein on hot metal. Ditto for toasting the hoagie roll.

FOR THE MEATBALLS

2 slices white bread (I leave on the crusts), cut into ½-inch (1 cm) dice (enough to make 1½ cups/45 g)

½ cup (120 ml) half-and-half or milk

1½ pounds (680 g) ground veal or a mixture of ground meats (such as veal, beef, pork, and/or chicken or turkey)

1 large shallot or ¼ onion, peeled and minced (about ¼ cup/35 g)

3 tablespoons minced fresh flat-leaf parsley or basil

1 teaspoon dried oregano

1 teaspoon coarse salt (sea or kosher), or to taste

½ teaspoon freshly ground black pepper or to taste

About 1 cup (3½ ounces/100 g) freshly and finely grated Parmigiano-Reggiano (optional)

TO FINISH THE PO' BOY

4 hoagie rolls

Extra virgin olive oil for the griddle

1 cup (240 ml) tomato sauce (preferably homemade, recipe follows), warmed

About ¾ cup (2⅔ ounces/75 g) freshly and finely grated Parmigiano-Reggiano (optional)

8 ounces (225 g) fontina or mozzarella cheese (see What's More), thinly sliced

YOU'LL ALSO NEED

A griddle press (or cast-iron skillet)

A griddle dome

1. Make the meatballs: Place the bread in a large mixing bowl and stir in the half-and-half. Let stand for 5 minutes.

2. Pour off the excess half-and-half. Add the ground meat, shallot, parsley, oregano, salt, pepper, and grated cheese

(recipe continues)

(if using). Mix well with a wooden spoon or your fingers. To test the meatballs for seasoning, fry a small ball on a hot griddle or in a small skillet until cooked, then taste it. The mixture should be highly seasoned— add salt and pepper as needed.

3. Form the meatballs: Dampen your hands with cold water. Pinch off 2-inch (5 cm) portions of the mixture and roll them into balls between your palms. Place on a plate lined with plastic wrap and refrigerate, covered with more plastic wrap, until cooking (they'll keep for up to 6 hours).

4. When ready to make the po' boys, heat your griddle or plancha with three zones: one on high for cooking the meatballs, one on medium for toasting the rolls, and one zone on low for warming. Oil it well.

5. Arrange the meatballs on the high zone of the griddle and flatten slightly with a griddle press. Cook the meatballs until sizzling and browned on the bottom, 2 to 3 minutes. Turn and cook

the other side the same way until cooked through, 5 to 6 minutes in all. Slide the meatballs to the low zone to keep warm.

6. Meanwhile, cut the hoagie rolls lengthwise from the top nearly to the bottom and spread open the two halves like a book. (If you prefer, cut them through completely.) Re-oil the medium zone, if necessary, and brown the cut sides of the rolls there, 1 minute. (It doesn't hurt to mop up the meatball fat.)

7. Pile the meatballs onto the toasted hoagie rolls. Spoon tomato sauce over them. Sprinkle each with one-fourth of the grated Parmigiano-Reggiano, if using, and lay the fontina or mozzarella slices on top.

8. Return the po' boys to the medium zone of the griddle and cover with a griddle dome. Cook until the cheese is melted and the sauce bubbles, 2 minutes. Take care not to burn the bottom of the bread. Dig in!

WHAT ELSE There are probably as many different meatball recipes as there are Italian grandmothers. The basic elements are the ground meat(s), binder, and seasonings. I'm partial to ground veal or a mixture of veal, beef, and pork, but any of these, or even others, like ground turkey or chicken, will get you over the finish line. I'm not going to tell you to make your tomato sauce from scratch (extra points if you do), but do use a good commercial brand your grandmother would approve of. Your grandmother wouldn't approve? Make it from scratch— see page 88.

WHAT'S MORE Try to buy fresh mozzarella (the kind that comes packed in liquid). The flavor and texture will be better. Alternatively, use Italian fontina, which is "meltier" and gives you more of a cheese pull than fresh mozzarella.

QUICK MADE-FROM-SCRATCH TOMATO SAUCE

MAKES 1¾ CUPS (415 ML)

Having gone to the trouble of making meatballs from scratch, perhaps you'll want to do the same with your tomato sauce. Here's my go-to recipe, which uses olives and capers for extra flavor.

---

2 tablespoons extra virgin olive oil

1 small onion, peeled and minced

2 cloves garlic, peeled and minced

1 teaspoon dried oregano

½ to 1 teaspoon hot red pepper flakes

2 tablespoons brined capers, drained

¼ cup (35 g) chopped pitted black olives

1 can (14 ounces/395 g) peeled whole tomatoes with juices (preferably fire-roasted tomatoes, like Muir Glen)

Freshly ground black pepper

6 fresh basil leaves, slivered

---

1. Heat the olive oil in a saucepan over medium-high heat. Add the onion, garlic, oregano, and hot red pepper flakes and cook over high heat until fragrant and golden, 3 minutes, stirring with a wooden spoon. Stir in the capers and olives and cook for 1 minute.

2. Stir in the tomatoes with their juices and simmer until richly flavored, 5 minutes. Using two knives in a scissor-like motion, cut the tomatoes into bite-size pieces (or you can chop them up with the edge of the wooden spoon). Stir in freshly ground pepper and basil.

Griddle Feast

A DINER LUNCH

The diner is a uniquely American institution—born from the horse-drawn lunch wagons of the 19th century, reaching its apotheosis in the sleek stainless-steel Art Deco diners of the 1930s. And the focal point of the diner kitchen was and is, you guessed it, the griddle. Think of diner menu classics: the BLT, the grilled cheese sandwich (technically speaking, a *griddled* cheese sandwich), the slider, the juicy Lucy—all owe their lusciousness, not to mention their quick delivery, to the griddle.

Here's what's on the menu:

- BLT and Company (page 66)

- Grilled Cheese and Then Some (page 68)

- "Hot" Dog, Really (Griddled with Jalapeños and Pepper Jack Cheese) (page 115)

- Smash Browns (aka Smashed Potatoes) (page 209)

- Peppered Pineapple with Mezcal Whipped Cream (page 233)

Here's how to sequence the preparation:

The night before:
- Boil and cool the potatoes for the smash browns.

Before the meal prep:
- Assemble the grilled cheese sandwich.

- Make the black pepper sugar for the pineapple. Slice the fruit.

- Measure out and assemble the ingredients for the other dishes on trays.

The actual cook (serve each dish sequentially as it comes off the griddle):
- Heat your griddle or plancha with one zone on medium-high, one on medium, and one on low for warming.

- Cook the bacon on the medium-high zone; assemble and serve the BLTs.

- Cook the smash browns in the bacon fat on the medium-high zone. Slide them to the warming zone.

- Cook the grilled cheese sandwiches on the medium-high zone and serve.

- Cook the "hot" dogs on the medium-high zone and serve with the smash browns on the side.

- Scrape your griddle clean. Grease it with butter. Turn one zone up to high and griddle the pineapple.

CHAPTER 4

BURGERS & SAUSAGES

In the beginning, there were hamburgers—sizzled to meaty awesomeness on the griddle. Then came the smash burger and steak au poivre burger. Elsewhere in *Project Griddle* we find kalbi burgers with Korean beef and seasonings, lamb sliders from Israel, and lemongrass-laced meatballs from Vietnam. Hotdogs are no strangers to griddles—and here they crank up the heat with jalapeño chiles.

SMASH BURGERS
WITH RAICHLEN'S SPECIAL SAUCE

MAKES 4 BURGERS

For years, I've extolled the virtues of cooking burgers on the grill (preferably over a wood fire), and for years I've inveighed against pressing those burgers with the flat part of a spatula (an act that squeezes the luscious meat juices onto the coals). But there's one burger that does better on a griddle than a grill and that absolutely thrives when pressed. You guessed it: the smash burger. The genius of the method lies in smashing the burger on hot flat metal, pressing out the fat, caramelizing the meat, and crisping the edges.

1½ pounds (680 g) ground beef, preferably 20 percent fat

Coarse salt (sea or kosher) and freshly ground black pepper

Canola or olive oil for the griddle

4 brioche buns, split

Raichlen's Special Sauce (recipe follows) or your favorite condiments

4 Boston lettuce leaves

1 luscious ripe red tomato, cut into ¼-inch (6 mm) slices

4 paper-thin slices sweet onion (optional) (See What's More on page 97.)

Dill or sweet pickle slices (optional)

YOU'LL ALSO NEED
A griddle press (or cast-iron skillet)
An instant-read thermometer (optional)

1. Form the beef into 8 even balls. Refrigerate until you're ready to cook.

2. Heat your griddle or plancha to high and lightly oil it.

3. Arrange the burger balls on the griddle, leaving 3 inches (8 cm) between them. Smash them with a griddle press until just shy of ¼ inch (6 mm) thick. Season the burgers with

salt and pepper. Cook until the burgers are sizzling and darkly browned on the bottom, 2 to 4 minutes. Use a spatula to invert the burgers, then place the griddle press on top and press hard. Continue griddling until both sides are browned, with crusty, lacy edges. Cook the burgers to taste—I like medium (160°F/71°C on an instant-read thermometer)—another 2 to 4 minutes.

(recipe continues)

4. Meanwhile, grill the cut sides of the buns on the plancha in the burger fat or with a little oil, 15 to 30 seconds.

5. To assemble the burgers, spread one of the bottom buns with special sauce.

Place a piece of lettuce on top. Top with 2 burgers, tomato, and onion and pickle slices, if using. Spread more special sauce on the cut side of the top bun and place on top. Dig in!

RAICHLEN'S SPECIAL SAUCE

MAKES ¾ CUP (180 ML)

2 tablespoons white miso, at room temperature, and/or 2 tablespoons Dijon mustard

6 tablespoons (85 g) mayonnaise (preferably Hellmann's)

2 tablespoons ketchup

1 to 2 tablespoons sriracha

½ teaspoon freshly ground black pepper

1 teaspoon sugar (optional)

Place the miso in a small mixing bowl. Add 1 tablespoon hot water and whisk until the miso dissolves. Stir in the remaining ingredients. Note: If you like your special sauce sweeter (I don't), add up to 1 teaspoon sugar.

WHAT ELSE Don't be afraid to press hard: You'll need the sustained pressure. Note: For an extra luxurious smash burger, use Wagyu beef (see page 140).

WHAT'S MORE We're not all fans of raw onion, so it's a good thing smash burgers and caramelized onions make good bedfellows. Make a batch following the instructions on page 97 and taste the magic.

BURGERS AU POIVRE

MAKES 4 BURGERS

Steak au poivre (peppercorn steak) is a French bistro classic. Michelin-starred chef Michael Beltran gives it the burger joint twist at his Miami restaurant, Brasserie Laurel, crusting thin, double smash burgers with cracked black peppercorns, serving them cheeseburger style with melted cave-aged Gruyère on butter-toasted brioche buns. Here's my version: The caramelized onions and griddled mushrooms are optional.

½ cup (80 g) whole black peppercorns

1½ pounds (680 g) ground sirloin (not too lean, 15 to 20 percent fat)

Butter, canola oil, or extra virgin olive oil for the griddle

Coarse salt (sea or kosher)

4 thin slices cave-aged Gruyère cheese (6 to 8 ounces/170 to 225 g)

2 tablespoons unsalted butter

4 brioche buns, split

Caramelized Onions (recipe follows; optional)

Griddled Shiitakes (recipe follows; optional)

YOU'LL ALSO NEED

A griddle press (or cast-iron skillet)

A griddle dome

An instant-read thermometer (optional)

1. Crack the peppercorns: Place them on a large cutting board. Place a few at a time under the edge of a cast-iron skillet and crack them, levering the skillet up and down by the handle. Each peppercorn should be broken into 6 to 8 pieces. Place the peppercorns in a shallow bowl.

2. Form the ground sirloin into 4 equal patties, each ¾ inch (2 cm) thick. Make a shallow dimple in the center of each burger with your thumb. Cover with plastic wrap and keep chilled until ready to cook and eat.

3. Heat your griddle or plancha to high. Lightly grease it with butter or oil.

(recipe continues)

4. Season each burger on both sides with salt. Dip each burger in the peppercorns on both sides to crust thickly.

5. Arrange the burgers on the griddle and cook until crusty and browned on the bottom, 2 to 4 minutes. Turn them over and cook for 1 minute, then smash them with a griddle press to a thickness of ½ inch (1 cm).

6. Lay a slice of Gruyère cheese atop each burger. Cover with a griddle dome and continue cooking until the cheese is melted and the burgers are cooked to taste, 2 to 4 minutes more for medium (160°F/71°C on an instant-read thermometer).

7. Meanwhile, melt the 2 tablespoons butter elsewhere on your griddle. Toast the cut sides of the brioche buns until crusty, 15 to 30 seconds.

8. To serve, place the burgers on the buns. Top with caramelized onions and/or mushrooms (if using) and serve at once. This is one burger you can serve with a fine red wine.

WHAT ELSE For the best results, you'll want to crack your peppercorns fresh. My assistant, Nancy Loseke, suggests cracking them in a heavy-duty resealable plastic bag so they don't scatter all over the place. The larger the peppercorn pieces, the spicier the burgers.

WHAT'S MORE The Brasserie Laurel tops its burgers with caramelized onions and demi-glace. The former are easy to make on a griddle (read on). The latter is a highly reduced beef stock—you can purchase it premade at gourmet shops.

CARAMELIZED ONIONS

MAKES ENOUGH FOR 4 BURGERS

2 tablespoons unsalted butter, or
    as needed

1 large sweet onion, peeled and
    thinly sliced crosswise

Heat your griddle or plancha to medium-high. Add the butter. When melted and sizzling, add the onions. Cook until the onions are soft and dark golden brown, stirring with a spatula, 5 to 8 minutes. Add butter as needed and lower the heat if necessary to keep the onions from sticking and burning.

GRIDDLED SHIITAKES

MAKES ENOUGH FOR 4 BURGERS

2 tablespoons unsalted butter, or
    as needed

8 shiitake mushrooms, stemmed

Coarse salt (sea or kosher) and
    freshly ground black pepper

1. Heat your griddle or plancha to medium-high. Add the butter. When melted and sizzling, add the shiitakes, cap side down. Cook until sizzling, soft, and browned, 3 to 5 minutes. Season with salt and pepper as the shiitakes cook.

2. Turn the shiitakes over and cook the other side the same way. Serve hot.

CHOPPED CHEESE SANDWICH

MAKES 2 SANDWICHES (CAN BE MULTIPLIED AS DESIRED)

Say "chopped cheese" to New Yorkers and their eyes will gleam with pleasure. Say it to just about anyone else on the planet, and you'll be greeted with a look of puzzlement. Born at the Blue Sky Deli (aka Hajji's Deli) in East Harlem, the chopped cheese is actually a chopped, griddle-fried hamburger lavished with onions and American cheese and served on a hoagie roll. Two respected foodie friends—Sam Sifton of the *New York Times* and my stepson Jake—informed me that no griddle book would be complete without a chopped cheese recipe. I read you, guys. Here it is.

---

12 ounces (340 g) ground beef, preferably 20 percent fat

Coarse salt (sea or kosher) and freshly ground black pepper

Adobo seasoning or garlic powder (optional)

3 tablespoons cold unsalted butter in a chunk for the griddle

2 hoagie or sub rolls, cut almost in half through the side

1 small onion, peeled and thinly sliced

4 slices American cheese

FOR SERVING

Mayonnaise (preferably Hellmann's)

Ketchup (optional)

Sliced red ripe tomatoes

Shredded or chopped iceberg lettuce

YOU'LL ALSO NEED

A griddle dome

---

1. Line a plate with plastic wrap. Form the meat into 4 equal patties, each about 3 ounces (85 g). Place the patties on the plate, cover with more plastic wrap, and refrigerate until ready to cook. (The patties can be made up to a day ahead.)

2. Heat your griddle or plancha to medium-high in one zone and low in another. Season the patties on both sides with salt, pepper, and adobo, if using. Impale the butter on a fork and rub some of it on the medium-high zone of the grill. Arrange the hoagie rolls, cut sides down, on the buttered section and toast the rolls until golden brown, 1 to 2 minutes. Move to the low zone to keep warm.

3. Melt the remainder of the butter on the high zone and add the burgers and onions, keeping them separate. Cook the burgers until nicely browned on the bottom, 3 to 4 minutes, then turn with an offset spatula and cook until browned on the second side, 1 to 2 minutes. Cook the onions at the same time, turning them occasionally with the spatula, until they've begun to soften and caramelize.

4. While the meat and onions cook, spread mayonnaise and ketchup, if using, on the toasted sides of the rolls.

5. Using the edge of the spatula, chop the beef patties into small bits. Mix in the onions. Continue frying the burgers and onions until sizzling and browned, 2 to 4 minutes.

6. Push the meat and onions into two piles, each about the same size and shape as the rolls. Top each pile with 2 slices of cheese. Place a griddle dome over the meat to ensure the cheese melts, 2 minutes.

7. Carefully transfer the cheese-topped meat mixture to the prepared buns. Top with sliced tomatoes and lettuce. Serve immediately.

WHAT ELSE The traditional seasoning for the hamburger is a spice blend from Puerto Rico called adobo. Its principal ingredients are salt, garlic powder, oregano, pepper, and cumin. You can probably find it at your local supermarket, but if not, plain garlic powder will get you close.

WHAT'S MORE To most New Yorkers, the formula for chopped cheese is sacrosanct. I'm not a New Yorker and I am a perennial tinkerer, so I imagine the following applications of the chopped cheese technique:

- **The Sheboygan:** Replace the hamburger with fresh bratwurst (removed from the casings) and the American cheese with sliced Wisconsin cheddar. Add sauerkraut in place of the lettuce and tomatoes.

- **The Santa Fe:** Substitute fresh chorizo for the hamburger and pepper Jack cheese for the American. Add roasted poblano chiles and top with Pico de Gallo (page 150).

- **The Italian:** Use Italian sausage (hot or sweet—your choice) instead of the hamburger and sliced aged provolone in place of the American cheese.

KALBI BURGERS
(IN THE STYLE OF KOREAN BEEF RIBS)

MAKES 4 BURGERS

Kalbi—thin-sliced, marinated, charcoal-grilled rib eye—is one of the glories of Korean cuisine, seared over charcoal grills built right into the table at grill parlors across Korea and the US. I've reconfigured the typical seasonings—salty soy sauce, nutty sesame oil, sweet sugar, tangy ginger, and garlic (lots of garlic) into an easy-to-eat burger. You get the same beefy richness, the same aromatics, but now you can enjoy them on a bun.

FOR THE BURGERS

1½ pounds (680 g) ground beef
  (not too lean, 15 to 20 percent fat)

2 cloves garlic, peeled and minced

2 teaspoons peeled and minced fresh
  ginger

1 scallion, trimmed, white and green
  parts minced

3 tablespoons soy sauce

2 tablespoons toasted sesame oil,
  plus more for the griddle

1 to 2 tablespoons sugar

Sea salt and freshly ground black pepper

FOR THE GOCHUJANG MAYO

¾ cup (170 g) mayonnaise
  (preferably Hellmann's)

2 tablespoons gochujang paste
  or sauce

FOR SERVING

4 brioche buns, split

2 tablespoons melted unsalted butter
  for toasting the buns (optional)

4 romaine lettuce leaves

1 cucumber, thinly sliced

YOU'LL ALSO NEED
An instant-read thermometer
  (optional)

1. Place the beef in a mixing bowl. Sprinkle with the garlic, ginger, scallion, soy sauce, sesame oil, and sugar, and salt and pepper. Stir to mix with a wooden spoon or with your fingers. (At this point, I like to fry a tiny meatball in a small skillet or on the corner of the griddle so I can taste the mixture for seasoning and adjust the salt and pepper as needed.) Form the beef mixture into 4 patties, each ¾ inch (2 cm) thick. Make a shallow dimple in the center of each burger with your thumb. Cover and refrigerate until cooking.

2. Make the gochujang mayo: Place the mayonnaise and gochujang in a small bowl and whisk until smooth.

3. Heat your griddle or plancha to high and oil it well.

4. Arrange the burgers on the griddle. Cook until sizzling and browned on both sides and the beef is cooked through, turning once with a spatula, 3 to 4 minutes per side. Use an instant-read meat thermometer to check for doneness, if you wish: The safe internal temperature for ground beef will be 160°F (71°C) degrees.

5. Meanwhile, brush the cut sides of the buns with melted butter (if using). Arrange on the griddle, cut side down, and cook until lightly toasted, 15 to 30 seconds.

6. Assemble the kalbi burgers: Spread the bun bottoms with some of the gochujang mayonnaise. Place a lettuce leaf on the lower half of the bun. Add a burger, then top with some cucumber slices. Top with the remaining gochujang mayo and the bun top. Dig in!

WHAT ELSE Gochujang is a Korean fermented chili paste. It's not overly fiery, but it's rich in umami flavors. You can find it at many supermarkets or at Asian markets. Gochujang sauce has a similar flavor but with a pourable consistency and a little sweetness. Both can be ordered online.

WHAT'S MORE These burgers take their name from Korea's celebrated beef short rib dish: kalbi. To make kalbi, substitute crosscut beef short ribs (sometimes called flanken) for the ground beef. Make a marinade by combining the garlic, ginger, and scallions in a mixing bowl. Stir in 1¼ cups (295 ml) soy sauce, 3 tablespoons of sesame oil, 2 tablespoons sugar, and 2 tablespoons mirin or sake. Marinate the beef ribs for 4 to 6 hours in the refrigerator. Drain well, then cook on the griddle or plancha as you would the hamburgers.

LAMB BURGER "HOAGIE"

MAKES 4 SANDWICHES

We North Americans don't eat a lot of ground lamb, but on vast swaths of the planet—from the Middle East to Central and Southern Asia, the lamb burger reigns supreme. This one features the timeless flavors of onion and parsley, with cucumber, tomato, and yogurt rounding out the roll. If you've never tried ground lamb, this is a great place to start, and if lamb just isn't your thing, a beef burger can be made the same way with equally tasty results.

1½ pounds (680 g) ground lamb

1 small onion, finely chopped

⅓ cup (20 g) finely chopped fresh flat-leaf parsley or mint

2 hoagie rolls

Canola or olive oil for the griddle

Coarse salt (sea or kosher) and freshly ground black pepper

4 lettuce leaves

1 cucumber (preferably Kirby), thinly sliced

1 luscious red ripe tomato, stemmed and thinly sliced

¾ cup (180 g) plain yogurt or Minted Yogurt (page 212)

---

1. Place the lamb in a mixing bowl and mix in the chopped onion and parsley with a wooden spoon or your fingers. Form the mixture into 8 small patties and place on a plate lined with plastic wrap. Refrigerate, covered with additional plastic wrap, until ready to cook (you can mix and form the lamb burgers up to 4 hours ahead).

2. Cut each hoagie roll in half widthwise. Cut each section almost in half through the side and open it like a book.

3. Just before serving, heat your griddle or plancha to high. Oil it well.

Season the lamb patties with salt and pepper on both sides. Arrange on the griddle and cook until browned on both sides, turning with a spatula, 2 to 3 minutes per side for medium, a little longer for medium-well.

4. Move the lamb burgers to the edge of the griddle and warm the bread, cut side down, where you cooked the lamb. Add oil as needed.

5. Arrange the lettuce leaves on the bread. Arrange the lamb burgers on top. Top with cucumber and tomato slices and a generous dollop of yogurt. Serve at once.

WHAT ELSE For the bread, use a hoagie roll or brioche bun. If you're using plain yogurt, and not the Minted Yogurt (page 212), it should be thick and unsweetened, like the Greek-style yogurts so abundant at the supermarket.

WHAT'S MORE This is the basic formula for lamb burgers. Other popular Middle East flavorings include chopped shelled pistachios, diced hot peppers, chopped tomatoes, poppy seeds—the possibilities are endless.

SIX WAYS TO ENHANCE YOUR BURGERS USING THE GENIUS OF A GRIDDLE

Most of the millions, dare I say billions, of burgers served in the United States are cooked on a griddle. Here's how to take yours over the top.

PROSCIUTTO "BACON" BURGERS: A great way to upscale your bacon burger. Use the Prosciutto Bacon on page 26.

CRISPY CHEESEBURGERS: Melted cheese atop a burger is good. Crispy melted cheese (or both!) is even better. Use the Manchego, Parmigiano-Reggiano, or cheddar cheese crisps on page 50.

PIMENTO CHEESEBURGERS: For a Southern touch, top your burger with the Pimento Cheese on page 84.

MIX YOUR MEATS: Consider adding lamb, veal, or pork to the beef. (If using two meats, combine half and half; if using three, combine in thirds.)

SMASH YOUR BURGERS: For crisp lacy edges and a luscious interior, smash your burger with your griddle press (see page 94).

TAPAS BAR BURGERS: Top your burger with shaved Manchego cheese and Tapas Bar Mushrooms (page 47). Serve with a glass of Spanish sherry.

ZUZU'S BEEF, LAMB, AND PINE NUT SLIDERS
WITH YOGURT AND TAHINI

SERVES 12 AS AN APPETIZER, 6 AS A MAIN COURSE

I'm sitting in a sleek, modern restaurant overlooking the Sea of Galilee, eating—make that feasting on—some of the best food I've had in decades. Welcome to Magdalena, located in Migdal (the birthplace of Mary Magdalene) and run by the godfather of Israeli Arab cuisine, Yousef "Zuzu" Hanna. Arab Christian by birth, Zuzu deftly weaves biblical foods and Arab culinary traditions into a cuisine that is simultaneously modern and ageless. The following sliders belong to a family of grilled ground meat dishes called kofta. Traditionally, the mixture would be grilled on skewers. I've turned it into sliders. Zuzu loads them with flavor thanks to the addition of onion, parsley, pepper, and cumin, with toasted pine nuts for crunch.

FOR THE BURGERS

2 pounds (910 g) lean ground beef, chilled

1 pound (455 g) ground lamb (not too lean), chilled

1 large onion, peeled and coarsely grated on a box grater

1 cup (60 g) finely chopped flat-leaf parsley

½ cup (70 g) toasted pine nuts

1 tablespoon freshly ground black pepper

1 tablespoon salt

1 teaspoon ground cumin

3 tablespoons extra virgin olive oil, plus more for the griddle

FOR SERVING

Small pita breads (optional)

1 cup (225 g) Greek-style yogurt, placed in a bowl and whisked until smooth

¾ cup (180 ml) tahini

---

1. Place the beef and lamb in a large mixing bowl (or in the bowl of an electric mixer fitted with a paddle). Knead well with your hands for 2 minutes to mix the meats.

2. Add the onion, parsley, pine nuts, pepper, salt, cumin, and the 3 tablespoons of olive oil and knead to mix. Cover the bowl and chill the mixture for 2 hours to blend the flavors.

(recipe continues)

3. Line a baking sheet with plastic wrap. Knead the meat mixture again (this repeated kneading gives you the springy texture prized by Galileans). Pinch off 2-inch (5 cm) balls and form them into patties about ½ inch (1 cm) thick. Arrange the patties on the baking sheet and refrigerate until serving.

4. Heat your griddle or plancha to high.

5. Lightly oil the griddle with olive oil. Arrange the meat patties on top and cook until sizzling and browned on both sides, 2 to 3 minutes per side. If using the pita breads, warm them on the griddle.

6. Transfer to a platter or plates and serve with yogurt and tahini drizzled on top. I like to serve them sandwich-style—2 or 3 patties to a pita—with yogurt and tahini spooned inside.

WHAT ELSE Adapted from Zuzu's handsome book, *The Galilee Table*, these beef, lamb, and pine nut sliders make a great party dish—especially when served sandwich-style in mini pita breads.

WHAT'S MORE The flavorings that make these sliders so vibrant go equally well with ground turkey or chicken. Tahini is sesame seed paste. Look for it at Middle Eastern markets and many supermarkets.

MUSA'S ADANA KEBAB
(CHILE-LACED LAMB "SLIDERS")

SERVES 4

There may be fancier or more famous restaurants in Istanbul. But none will teach you more about Turkish food culture than the trio of Ciya (pronounced Chee-ya) restaurants run by chef-turned-anthropologist and food historian, Musa Dağdeviren. Take a ferry to the Kadiköy district on Istanbul's Asian side and walk down an exuberantly colorful market street to Musa's flagship restaurant, Ciya Kebap. There you'll be greeted by an astonishing selection of traditional Anatolian soups, stews, salads, breads from a wood-burning oven, and kebabs from a charcoal-burning grill.

Adana kebab, fired up with hot pepper flakes and named for a city in southwest Anatolia, is one of Turkey's most popular kebabs. Musa's version incorporates both fresh and dried chiles for extra punch, not to mention a mincemeat made with three separate cuts of lamb (shoulder, brisket, and tail fat). I mention that for authenticity's sake, but conventional ground lamb delivers plenty of flavor. I like to serve this with a fresh mint-spiked Onion Tomato "Salsa." You can prep it beforehand or make it after forming the lamb patties.

1½ pounds (680 g) ground lamb (not too lean), chilled

1 small onion, finely chopped (⅔ cup/85 g)

1 fresh hot chile, such as a horn pepper, jalapeño, or serrano, minced (for milder Adana kebabs, seed the chiles)

1½ teaspoons coarse salt (sea or kosher)

1½ teaspoons freshly ground black pepper

1 to 2 teaspoons Aleppo pepper, Urfa pepper, or hot red pepper flakes

½ teaspoon ground cumin

2 tablespoons unsalted butter, at room temperature

Onion Tomato "Salsa" for serving (recipe follows)

Canola or olive oil for the griddle

Lavash or pita bread for serving

(recipe continues)

1. Place the lamb, onion, fresh chile, salt, pepper, hot red pepper flakes, cumin, and butter in a mixing bowl. Knead well with your fingers to mix or stir with a wooden spoon.

2. Pinch off 2-inch (5 cm) portions of the lamb mixture and roll them into balls. Gently flatten them into 2-inch (5 cm) patties. (It helps to oil your hands or wet them with cold water to keep the meat from sticking.) Transfer the patties to a sheet pan lined with plastic wrap and refrigerate until ready to cook.

3. Heat your griddle or plancha to high and oil it well. Fry the lamb patties until sizzling and browned on both sides and just cooked through, 2 to 3 minutes per side. Do not overcook, or the lamb will dry out.

4. Warm the lavash or pita breads in the lamb fat on the griddle. Serve the lamb patties wrapped in lavash with the Onion Tomato "Salsa" spooned over them.

WHAT ELSE Traditionally, Adana kebab comes molded on a skewer and grilled over charcoal. I give them the slider treatment here, and the griddle does a fine job of laying on a sizzling caramelized crust. To be strictly authentic, you'd use Urfa pepper (a dried hot red chile) from Turkey or Syrian-style Aleppo pepper. Hot pepper flakes work just fine.

WHAT'S MORE Another of Musa's kebabs features poppy seeds—a felicitous addition to these or any ground lamb kebabs. Two tablespoons would do the trick for this recipe. Sprinkle them on the outside of the meat patties just before griddling.

ONION TOMATO "SALSA"

MAKES 1½ TO 2 CUPS (405 TO 540 G)

This salsa-cum-relish-cum-salad accompanies all manner of grilled meats in Turkey, and the freshness of the tomatoes and mint have a welcome cooling effect on the fiery chiles in the kebabs. There's one special ingredient you'll need to know about—sumac—a reddish-purplish powder ground from a tart berry used throughout the Middle East. Look for it at Middle Eastern markets and many supermarkets or substitute a generous squeeze of fresh lemon juice.

---

2 large luscious red ripe tomatoes

1 small to medium sweet onion, peeled

½ red bell pepper, stemmed and seeded

¾ cup (40 g) roughly chopped flat-leaf parsley

6 fresh mint leaves, thinly sliced

2 teaspoons sumac

½ teaspoon sea salt

3 tablespoons extra virgin olive oil

Cut the tomatoes in half from top to bottom and thinly slice each half. Place the tomatoes with their juices in a mixing bowl. Cut the onion the same way. Thinly slice the bell pepper. Add them to the tomatoes with the parsley, mint, sumac, salt, and olive oil. Toss to mix, adding salt as needed to taste. Let stand for at least 10 minutes but not more than 1 hour before serving.

VIETNAMESE PORK MEATBALLS
(BUN CHA)

SERVES 8 TO 12 AS AN APPETIZER, 4 TO 6 AS A MAIN COURSE

Bun cha is Vietnam's answer to Middle Eastern kofta (page 105) or Swedish meatballs. The meat in question is pork—laced with rice noodles and that quartet of Southeast Asian flavorings: shallots, garlic, cilantro, and lemongrass. Fish sauce provides the salt, while sugar adds a note of sweetness. And if that's not flavorful enough, you serve the meatballs with fresh mint, basil leaves, and sliced chiles, the whole shebang wrapped in lettuce leaves and dipped in a sweet-salty sauce flavored with fish sauce, garlic, and lime juice. Bun cha makes a killer party dish, with guests customizing their servings to taste.

2 ounces (60 g) dried rice vermicelli (optional)

1 shallot, peeled and roughly chopped

2 cloves garlic, peeled and roughly chopped

2 stalks lemongrass, trimmed and roughly chopped

¼ cup (15 g) fresh cilantro leaves, roughly chopped

2 teaspoons freshly ground black pepper

3 tablespoons sugar

2 pounds (910 g) ground pork, chilled

¼ cup (60 ml) fish sauce (use a Vietnamese brand like Three Crabs or Red Boat)

Canola or olive oil for the griddle

FOR SERVING

1 head Bibb or Boston lettuce, broken into leaves, washed and spun dry

1 bunch fresh mint, torn into sprigs

1 bunch fresh Thai basil or regular basil, torn into sprigs

Cilantro sprigs

1 to 2 serrano or jalapeño chiles, thinly sliced (optional)

Nuoc Cham (recipe follows)

YOU'LL ALSO NEED

A food processor

(recipe continues)

1. If using the rice noodles, place them in a bowl with cold water to cover. Let soften for 1 hour. Drain well. Using kitchen scissors, cut the rice noodles into 1-inch (3 cm) pieces.

2. Make the meatballs: Place the shallot, garlic, lemongrass, chopped cilantro, pepper, and sugar in a food processor. Process until very finely chopped.

3. Place the pork in a large mixing bowl. Add the shallot mixture, noodles, if using, and fish sauce and knead or stir until well mixed. Cover with plastic wrap and refrigerate for 1 to 2 hours to let the flavors infuse and firm up the meat.

4. Line a sheet pan with plastic wrap. Pinch off 1-inch (3 cm) portions of the pork mixture and roll them into balls. Gently flatten them into 1-inch (3 cm) patties. (It helps to oil your hands or wet them with cold water to keep the meat from sticking.) Transfer the patties to the sheet pan and refrigerate until cooking.

5. Arrange the garnishes on a platter with a small bowl of Nuoc Cham (dipping sauce) for each eater.

6. Heat your griddle or plancha to high and oil it well. Cook the pork patties until sizzling and browned on both sides and just cooked through, 1 to 2 minutes per side. Do not overcook, or the meatballs will dry out.

7. To serve, place a pork patty or two on a lettuce leaf. Top it with some sprigs of mint, basil, and cilantro, and sliced chiles, if using. Roll it up and dip in the Nuoc Cham. Pop it into your mouth and get ready for gustatory fireworks.

WHAT ELSE Traditionally, bun cha would be grilled, but the griddle does a great job of searing the meat and caramelizing the sugar. I've made the thin rice noodles optional, but they do add an interesting texture. (In a pinch, you could substitute cooked angel hair spaghetti or soba.) To trim lemongrass, cut off the green part (the top two-thirds) and the root end. Peel off the outside leaves of what remains. If lemongrass is unavailable, substitute ½ teaspoon freshly and finely grated lemon zest. Note: This recipe is simple and straightforward, but it does require some extra time for soaking the rice noodles and chilling the meatballs. Figure on 3 hours start to finish, with not more than 30 minutes actual cooking time.

NUOC CHAM

MAKES ABOUT 1 CUP (270 G)

Vietnamese meatballs and other griddled and grilled meats are traditionally served with a sweet, sour, garlicky, salty dipping sauce called nuoc cham. Here's how you make it.

---

1 carrot, peeled

3 tablespoons sugar

2 cloves garlic, peeled and minced

¼ cup (60 ml) fresh lime juice

¼ cup (60 ml) fish sauce

3 tablespoons rice vinegar

1 serrano or Thai chile (preferably red), cut widthwise into paper-thin slices

---

1. Using a vegetable peeler, cut 4 paper-thin strips of carrot. Pile these strips one on top of the other and, using a sharp chef's knife, cut lengthwise into paper-thin threads. Place these in a small bowl. (Eat the rest of the carrot. ☺) Stir in 1 tablespoon of the sugar and let stand until the carrot threads soften, 10 minutes.

2. Place the garlic and remaining sugar in the bottom of a nonreactive mixing bowl. Mash together with the back of a spoon. Add the lime juice, fish sauce, and rice vinegar, and stir until the sugar is dissolved. Stir in the carrot mixture and enough water to make a mellow, well-balanced sauce (you will probably need about 4 tablespoons/60 ml). Taste the sauce for seasoning: It should be sweet, sour, salty, and aromatic.

3. Divide the sauce among four small serving bowls. Sprinkle each with thinly sliced chiles.

"HOT" DOG, REALLY
(GRIDDLED WITH JALAPEÑOS AND PEPPER JACK CHEESE)

MAKES 4 HOTDOGS, SERVES 2 TO 4

The hotdog is a cookout mainstay—prized as much for its ease of preparation as for its rich, smoky, garlicky taste. So how could you possibly improve on a sausage that comes already cooked, requiring nothing more than reheating? By dividing and conquering—that's how. Namely, by slicing the hotdog nearly in half lengthwise so you can open it up like a book. Thus butterflied, the hotdog presents double the surface area you can cook to a crusty brown. More crust and more browning means more Maillard effect and that means more flavor. And nothing does it better than a griddle. But I like to go one step further, making a hotdog that lives up to its name: hot. Enter griddled jalapeños, pepper Jack cheese, and horseradish mustard spiked with sriracha. Now *that's* what I call a "hot" dog.

FOR THE DOGS

4 of your favorite hotdogs

Canola or olive oil for the griddle

4 jalapeño chiles, thinly sliced on the diagonal (see What Else)

4 to 6 ounces (115 to 170 g) pepper Jack cheese, thinly sliced

FOR SERVING

4 brioche hotdog rolls, split

⅔ cup (160 g) sauerkraut (optional)

Horseradish mustard (or your favorite mustard) in a squeeze bottle

Sriracha in a squeeze bottle

YOU'LL ALSO NEED

A griddle press (or cast-iron skillet)

A griddle dome (optional)

---

1. Heat your griddle or plancha to medium-high with one zone on low.

2. Using a chef's knife, cut each hotdog almost in half lengthwise. Open it up like a book and gently press it open so it lies flat.

3. Lightly oil the griddle. Lay the hotdogs, cut side down, on the medium-high zone of the griddle and place a griddle press on top. Cook until sizzling and browned on the bottom, 2 minutes.

(recipe continues)

4. At the same time, arrange the jalapeño slices on the griddle and cook, turning with a spatula, until sizzling and browned on both sides, 1 to 2 minutes per side.

5. Invert the hotdogs and arrange the griddled jalapeño slices on top. Top with pepper Jack cheese slices. Cook until the dogs are sizzling and browned on the outside and the cheese is melted, 2 to 4 minutes more. Note: To facilitate melting the cheese, you can place a griddle dome on top. Move the hotdogs off to a cooler part of the griddle to keep warm.

6. Grill the hotdog rolls, cut side down, in the hotdog fat until browned, 30 to 60 seconds.

7. To assemble, place a hotdog with its topping on a roll. Top with sauerkraut (if using). Squirt squiggles of mustard and sriracha on top and dig in!

WHAT ELSE There are many hotdog varieties to choose from: Hebrew National (my personal favorite), Ball Park, even costly Wagyu hotdogs made from Japanese-style beef. For hotter "hot" dogs, leave the jalapeño seeds in. For milder dogs, seed the jalapeños, or use a milder chile, like a poblano.

Griddle Feast

A TAILGATE PARTY

Tailgating has been an American institution for more than a century—since 1869 to be precise, when Rutgers and Princeton played their first intercollegiate football game near New Brunswick, New Jersey. Spectators gathered before the game, serving picnic lunches from the tailgates of their horse-drawn wagons. Imagine what would be their surprise at seeing modern tailgating, with its elaborate outdoor kitchens and military-strength audiovisual systems. Today, more than 20 million Americans participate in these boisterous stadium parking lot parties, and millions more host the get-togethers at their own homes. The following will help you up your game at the griddle.

Here's what's on the menu:

- Tortillas con Queso Fundido (Griddled Cheese and Chorizo Tortillas) (page 127)

- Chicken Fingers for Grown-ups (page 162)

- The Midnighter (Cuban Ham, Cheese, Pork, and Pickle Sandwich) (page 74)

- Muffuletta (Hot New Orleans Cold Cut Sandwich) (page 77)

- Smash Burgers with Raichlen's Special Sauce (page 92)

Here's how to sequence the preparation:

Before the game prep:

- Assemble the midnighters.

- Assemble the muffulettas.

- Measure out and assemble the ingredients for the other dishes on trays.

The actual cook (serve each dish sequentially as it comes off the griddle):

- Heat your griddle or plancha with one zone on medium-high, one on medium, and one on medium-low. Oil the griddle.

- Assemble, cook, and serve the tortillas con queso fundido on the medium-high and medium-low zones.

- Assemble, cook, and serve the chicken fingers on the medium-high zone.

- Cook and serve the midnighters on the medium-high zone.

- Cook and serve the muffulettas on the medium zone.

- Turn the medium-high zone up to high. Cook and serve the smash burgers on the high zone.

Game on!

CHAPTER 5

FLATBREADS & TORTILLA DISHES

Long before there were ovens, people "baked" their breads on flat fire-heated stones. Which evolved into flat clay skillets called comals. Which evolved into metal griddles. And despite advances in the baker's art, such as gas and electric ovens, the griddle remains the cooker of choice for many of the world's great flatbreads. Consider Mexico's tortilla, for example. Or Venezuela's arepa. Or Italy's piadina. Get ready for:

SMOKED PAPRIKA GARLIC BREAD

SERVES 3 OR 4

I like to think of this as garlic bread with a Spanish accent. The pimentón (smoked paprika) adds an earthy smokiness. You can slice the baguette sharply on the diagonal into what I call rabbit ears. Or cut it lengthwise into long thin slices. If you have a griddle press, use it to press the bread slices into the hot olive oil on the griddle. Otherwise, use the bottom of a cast-iron skillet. Pressing the bread makes it extra crackly crisp.

---

3 tablespoons unsalted butter

2 tablespoons extra virgin olive oil, plus more for the griddle

1 or 2 cloves garlic, peeled and minced

1 scallion, trimmed and minced (reserve 2 tablespoons scallion greens for garnish)

1 baguette

Pimentón for sprinkling

Coarse sea salt (optional—most bread contains enough salt)

YOU'LL ALSO NEED

A pastry brush

A griddle press (or cast-iron skillet)

---

1. Heat your griddle or plancha to medium-high.

2. Heat the butter and 2 tablespoons of the olive oil in a small saucepan on the griddle until the butter melts. Add the garlic and scallion and cook until fragrant and just beginning to brown, 2 minutes. Immediately remove the pan from the heat. Note: You can also do this on your stovetop.

3. Using a serrated knife and working from top to bottom, cut the baguette sharply on the diagonal into ½-inch-thick (1 cm) slices. Using a pastry brush, generously paint the bread slices on both sides with the garlic scallion mixture. Thickly sprinkle each slice on both sides with pimentón and salt to taste.

4. Oil the griddle with olive oil. Arrange the bread slices on the griddle and place a griddle press on top to press the bread onto the hot metal. Cook until sizzling and browned on both sides, 2 to 3 minutes per side.

5. Serve hot off the griddle, sprinkled with scallion greens.

WHAT ELSE I like to use a mixture of butter (for richness) and extra virgin olive oil (for taste). You can use solely one or the other. Pimentón is available sweet or hot. Look for it at Spanish markets and many supermarkets. If unavailable, use Hungarian sweet or hot paprika.

WHAT'S MORE

- **To make pa amb tomàquet (Catalan tomato bread),** rub each slice of hot garlic bread with chunks of juicy ripe red tomato. Better yet, give your guests fresh tomato chunks and have them do the rubbing.

- **To make blue cheese garlic bread,** add 3 tablespoons room temperature Roquefort, Gorgonzola, or other blue cheese to the garlic scallion mixture. Spread this on the bread slices and griddle as directed.

- **To make parmesan garlic bread,** sprinkle the buttered bread slices with finely grated Parmigiano-Reggiano cheese.

JALAPEÑO CHEDDAR AREPAS

MAKES 6

Cross a Rhode Island johnnycake (a crisp cornmeal pancake) with a Mexican white corn tortilla, and you get Venezuela's national flatbread: the arepa. Milder and sweeter than tortillas, arepas are softly crusty on the outside, fluffy-creamy inside, and absolutely irresistible. Miami, where I live, is home to a large Venezuelan community, so these small round cakes (about the size of an English muffin half) turn up at lunch counters, street fairs, farmers' markets, and yes, premade, in our local supermarkets. By themselves, they're somewhat bland (think the flavor and texture of cream of wheat), but stuffed with cheese, picadillo (spiced ground beef), and numerous other fillings, they become addictive. Here, arepas get the cheese treatment with cheddar, jalapeño, and scallion.

---

1 cup (160 g) arepa flour (see What Else)

¼ teaspoon coarse salt (sea or kosher), or to taste

1¼ cups (295 ml) cool water, or as needed

About 1 cup (4 ounces/115 g) coarsely grated sharp white cheddar cheese

1 jalapeño chile, seeded and minced

2 scallions, white and green parts trimmed and minced, or ½ cup (20 g) finely chopped fresh cilantro

Extra virgin olive oil or canola oil for the griddle

Butter for serving (optional)

---

1. Make the arepas: Place the arepa flour and salt in a large mixing bowl. Add the water, cheese, jalapeño, and scallions or cilantro. Stir to mix with a wooden spoon, then knead with your fingers until the mixture is smooth, 1 to 2 minutes. The consistency should resemble Play-Doh. Add a little more water if needed.

2. Cover with plastic wrap and let the mixture rest for 5 minutes.

3. Divide the mixture into 6 equal portions and roll each into a ball. Flatten each ball between the palms of your hands, then, with your fingers, make 6 round cakes, each about 3 inches (8 cm) in diameter and ⅓ inch (8 mm) thick.

4. Line a plate with plastic wrap and arrange the arepas on top. Cover with more plastic wrap and store in the refrigerator until ready to cook. The arepas can be formed several hours ahead.

5. When ready to serve, heat your griddle or plancha to medium and oil it well. Arrange the arepas on the griddle and cook until sizzling and lightly browned on the outside and heated through, 2 to 3 minutes per side. Serve at once. (I wouldn't say no to a pat of butter on top.)

WHAT ELSE Arepas are super easy to make, requiring nothing more than arepa flour and water. The former is a powdery flour made from precooked white corn kernels. (In this, arepas differ from tortillas, which are made with uncooked ground corn.) Look for arepa flour online, in Latin markets, and in the international aisle of larger supermarkets. The most famous Venezuelan brand is P.A.N.

WHAT'S MORE Of course, the easiest way to enjoy arepas is as Venezuelans do—without the cheese and other flavorings. Prepare as directed, omitting the cheese, jalapeños, and scallions. Cook on the griddle and serve with salted butter.

PIADINA
(ITALIAN MORTADELLA "QUESADILLA")

MAKES 2

Italy and Mexico lie an ocean and sea apart, but the two share a dish with an uncanny resemblance. I'm sure you know the Mexican quesadilla. Less familiar, perhaps, is Italy's piadina. Born in Emilia-Romagna, where it began as a simple flatbread cooked on a terra-cotta griddle (called a piastra) over wood embers, the piadina has evolved into a pan-Italian fast food. It starts with a white flatbread that looks for all the world like a flour tortilla. (Both contain white flour, water, and lard, but piadina also contains a little baking powder.) Inside, you'll find melted cheese, which in Italy might be stracciatella (a gooey, spoonable cheese, like the inside of a burrata), scamorza (smoked mozzarella), provola, fontina, or another Italian cheese. Unlike its Mexican counterpart, piadina also contains salumi (Italian cold cuts), such as thinly sliced prosciutto, speck (smoked prosciutto), mortadella, or one of Italy's hundreds of salamis. The crowning touch: a handful of cool, crisp, peppery arugula. It's a quesadilla Italian-style, and you'll definitely want to add it to your repertoire.

Olive oil for the griddle

2 large (8-inch/20 cm) flour tortillas

2 to 4 teaspoons Calabrian chili paste (optional, see What Else)

4 ounces (115 g) of any of the following cheeses: stracciatella, scamorza, provola, fontina, pecorino Romano, or other Italian cheese

3 to 4 ounces (85 to 115 g) thinly sliced mortadella, prosciutto, speck, or other Italian salume

2 generous handfuls fresh arugula

YOU'LL ALSO NEED
Parchment paper

1. Heat your griddle or plancha to medium-high and oil it well.

2. Meanwhile, arrange the tortillas on your work surface. Spread a little Calabrian chili paste on each (if using).

Don't use more than you mean to: This stuff is hot! If using stracciatella, spread it on each tortilla. If using another cheese, thinly slice or coarsely grate and arrange it on top of each tortilla. Top with the mortadella or

(recipe continues)

other salume. Top each with a piece of parchment paper just large enough to cover the tortilla.

3. Arrange the piadinas on the hot griddle, parchment paper side down. Cook until the meat is sizzling and browned, 1 to 2 minutes.

4. Use a spatula to invert the tortillas and peel off the parchment paper. Cook until the bottom of the tortilla is sizzling and browned, 1 to 2 minutes.

5. Transfer the piadinas to plates. Top each with a generous pile of arugula. Fold in half and dig in.

WHAT ELSE A purist may wish to make the piadina (flatbread) itself by hand: You'll find an excellent recipe in *The Splendid Table* by Lynne Rossetto Kasper. But honestly, it's so similar to a flour tortilla, you might as well save time and use that. Calabrian chili paste (optional) is Italy's most fiery condiment—one good brand is L'Oro Del Sud (available on Amazon.com).

WHAT'S MORE Like quesadillas, piadinas are infinitely customizable. A piadina parlor I visited in the baroque city of Lecce in southern Italy proposed eight kinds of meat, a dozen kinds of cheeses, and vegetables ranging from asparagus to zucchini. While I love the crisp, cool crunch of the arugula against the melty hot cheese and salume, I also like two other traditional toppings: sautéed broccoli rabe and sautéed chard.

TORTILLAS CON QUESO FUNDIDO
(GRIDDLED CHEESE AND CHORIZO TORTILLAS)

**MAKES 2, SERVES 3 OR 4 AS AN APPETIZER,
1 OR 2 AS A LIGHT MAIN COURSE**

Queso fundido is Mexico's answer to Swiss fondue—cheese melted in the oven until bubbling in a cazuela (earthenware dish), to be scooped up with crisp tortilla chips. This "melted cheese" takes inspiration from the original but dispenses with the cazuela, instead melting the cheese directly onto crisp tortillas. And to gild the lily, as it were, add a spicy, sizzling layer of chorizo. It's not strictly traditional, but I think you'll love it.

Canola or olive oil for the griddle

12 ounces (2 links/340 g) raw chorizo (if using link sausages, remove the meat from the casings)

2 large (8-inch/20 cm) flour tortillas

About 2 cups (8 ounces/225 g) coarsely grated Oaxaca, Chihuahua, cheddar, Jack, or pepper Jack cheese

2 teaspoons dried oregano (preferably Mexican)

YOU'LL ALSO NEED
A griddle dome

---

1. Heat your griddle or plancha so that one zone is medium-high and one zone medium-low. Lightly oil the griddle.

2. Place 4 ounces (115 g) of chorizo on each tortilla and spread it out evenly with a spatula or the back of a spoon. Arrange the tortillas chorizo side down on the medium-high zone of the griddle. Cook until the chorizo is sizzling and browned, 2 to 4 minutes.

(recipe continues)

3. Invert the tortillas onto the medium-low zone and carefully arrange the grated cheese on top of the cooked chorizo. Sprinkle with oregano. Cover the tortillas with a griddle dome. Cook until the tortillas are crisp and brown on the bottom and the cheese is melted and bubbly, 2 to 4 minutes more.

4. Serve the tortillas con queso fundido whole or cut into wedges.

WHAT ELSE There are several options for cheese. Tradition calls for Oaxaca or Chihuahua cheese from Mexico—both excellent melting cheeses and available at Mexican markets and upscale supermarkets. For a north of the border touch, use pepper Jack, Monterey Jack, or white cheddar. This recipe couldn't be quicker or easier, but it does require one piece of equipment: a griddle dome, metal bowl, or a wok lid to hold in the heat to melt the cheese.

WHAT'S MORE For more elaborate tortillas con queso fundido, place a layer of sliced black olives and/or sliced pickled jalapeños under the cheese. To make a Wisconsin version, substitute fresh (uncooked) bratwurst for the chorizo and use sharp cheddar cheese. Yeah, you could brush the tortilla with German-style mustard before spreading the bratwurst, and I wouldn't say no to a thin layer of well-drained sauerkraut under the cheese.

ALMOST KHACHAPURI
(GEORGIAN-STYLE EGG AND CHEESE TORTILLA)

MAKES 1 (CAN BE MULTIPLIED AS DESIRED)

Khachapuri burst on the American food scene a few years ago, and it's been riding high ever since. Described as Georgian pizza (as in the Republic of Georgia), traditional khachapuri is a Caucasus Mountain–region delicacy consisting of a yeasted dough "canoe" loaded with tangy cheese and eggs and baked until sizzling in a wood-burning oven. An unlikely candidate, perhaps, for a griddle makeover, yet here I am riffing on the flavors and fillings by griddling a flour tortilla topped with a ring of grated feta and a sunny-side up egg in the center. The secret: Work on two heat zones and use a griddle dome to cook the egg. Almost Khachapuri makes a unique breakfast and a great dish for brunch or lunch.

Olive oil for the griddle

1 large (8-inch/20 cm) flour tortilla

About ¾ cup (3 ounces/85 g) coarsely grated sharp meltable cheese (see What Else)

1 large egg (preferably organic)

Dried oregano for sprinkling

Hot red pepper flakes, to taste

YOU'LL ALSO NEED
A griddle dome

---

1. Heat your griddle or plancha so that one zone is medium and one zone is low. Oil the medium zone with olive oil.

2. Place the tortilla on the medium zone and cook until the bottom is crisp and browned, 2 to 3 minutes.

3. Invert the tortilla with a spatula and slide it onto the low zone. Form a ring of grated cheese around the periphery of the tortilla and crack an egg in the center. Sprinkle with dried oregano.

4. Re-oil the medium zone and slide the tortilla there. Cover with a griddle dome. Cook until the cheese is melted, the egg is just set, and the bottom of the tortilla is crisp and browned, 4 to 6 minutes, or as needed. Sprinkle with hot red pepper flakes and serve.

(recipe continues)

WHAT ELSE The traditional cheeses for khachapuri are tangy imeruli and sulguni, but they're difficult to find in the US. In my book *How to Grill Vegetables*, I used a mixture of feta and Monterey Jack, and I recommend the same combo here. Lacking these, I make this recipe with sharp cheddar, and the results are sensational. Any sharp meltable cheese will do.

WHAT'S MORE Tradition calls for the khachapuri to be cooked open face, so the egg stays a little runny. You can serve the Almost Khachapuri this way, and it will be delectable. If you like your egg a little more cooked, re-oil the medium zone and invert the tortilla over it one more time. You may lose a little cheese, but the flavorful top crust is worth it.

And while we're reimagining traditional dishes, I suppose you could top the tortilla with a ring of chunky, spicy tomato sauce. Crack an egg in the center and cook as directed. It's a griddled shakshuka. You saw it here first!

TOTOPOS
(TORTILLA CRISPS)

SERVES 4

Born of the Zapotec peoples in Mexico's Oaxacan region, these flat corn crisps are perfect for breaking into pieces and dipping into salsa, or topping with refried beans or griddled beef or seafood to make tostadas (page 134). Tradition calls for forming totopos by hand, but packaged tortillas work just fine, too. Tradition also calls for cooking the totopos on a comal—a sort of flat frying pan. In other words, a griddle, which crisps the tortillas quickly and evenly—without the excess fat associated with deep-frying. Transfer the totopos to a wire rack, where they'll crisp on cooling.

---

4 medium (6-inch/15 cm) or 8 small
   (4-inch/10 cm) corn or flour tortillas

2 tablespoons extra virgin olive oil or
   melted unsalted butter, or as needed

Coarse salt (sea or kosher)

YOU'LL ALSO NEED
A wire cooling rack

---

1. Heat your griddle or plancha to medium-high.

2. Brush the tortillas on both sides with oil or butter and lightly season on both sides with salt to taste.

3. Arrange on the griddle and cook until crisp and lightly browned on both sides, 1 to 2 minutes per side. Transfer to a wire rack: They'll crisp on cooling.

WHAT ELSE Totopos can be made with white or yellow corn tortillas—or with flour tortillas. Stored in a sealed plastic container (once completely cool), they'll keep for up to a week. They never last more than a day in my house.

WHAT'S MORE

- **To make cheese totopos,** brush flour tortillas with extra virgin olive oil. Cook until the bottom is sizzling and browned, 1 to 2 minutes. Invert the tortilla and sprinkle the top with freshly and finely grated Parmigiano-Reggiano cheese.

- **To make garlic herb totopos,** brush the tortillas on both sides with melted unsalted butter and sprinkle both sides with minced garlic, parsley, basil, and/or chives. Griddle as directed.

- **To make totopos in the style of Chinese scallion pancakes,** use flour tortillas and brush them on both sides with toasted sesame oil. Sprinkle on both sides with thinly slivered scallion greens and sesame seeds. Griddle as directed.

- **To make dessert totopos,** brush flour tortillas on both sides with melted unsalted butter. Sprinkle both sides with cinnamon sugar. Griddle as directed.

TOSTADAS

(OPEN-FACE CRISPY TORTILLAS THREE WAYS)

MAKES 4, SERVES 1 OR 2 AS A MAIN COURSE
(CAN BE MULTIPLIED AS DESIRED)

In the pantheon of open face sandwiches, Mexico's tostada stands apart—singular in its simplicity, yet as complex as any Danish smørrebrød, combining the crunch of a tortilla chip with the gustatory pyrotechnics of a taco. At its most basic, it's little more than a tortilla—griddled until crisp, then topped with your favorite flavorings. At our house, that often means cooked beans (black or pinto—plus chiles, cheese, sour cream, and tomatoes) for a quick and simple dinner for Meatless Monday. If you want to mix things up, try one of the alternative fillings that follow (sub them in for the beans).

---

4 medium (6-inch/15 cm) corn tortillas (yellow or white—preferably artisanal)

1 to 2 tablespoons extra virgin olive oil or vegetable oil, plus oil for the beans and the griddle

1 small onion, peeled and diced

1 can (15 ounces/425 g) black or kidney beans, drained, rinsed, and drained again (see Note)

¼ teaspoon ground cumin

ANY OR ALL OF THE FOLLOWING TOPPINGS (AS MUCH OR AS LITTLE AS YOU LIKE)

Sour cream

Diced or sliced avocado (sprinkle with a few drops of lime juice to keep it from discoloring)

Thinly sliced jalapeño or serrano chile

Diced red tomato

Thinly sliced scallion (or diced red onion)

Roughly chopped fresh cilantro

Crumbled or coarsely grated Cotija or other tangy cheese

---

1. Heat your griddle or plancha to medium-high.

2. If using black beans, heat 1 tablespoon oil in a small skillet on the griddle. Add the onion and cook until lightly browned, 3 to 6 minutes, stirring often. Stir in the beans and cumin and cook until hot, 2 minutes. If using refried beans, cook the onions alone then warm them in a skillet on the griddle. Keep the beans warm at the edge of the griddle.

3. Brush the tortillas on both sides with olive oil. Have the other ingredients ready for the tostadas.

4. Arrange the tortillas on the griddle. Cook until browned and crisp on both sides, about 1 minute per side.

5. Transfer the crisp tortillas to a platter or plates. Top with the beans, sour cream, avocado, chiles, and any of the other toppings you desire.

Note: Feel free to replace the black beans with 1 cup (260 g) of your favorite refried beans (in which case, omit the cumin).

WHAT ELSE The toppings for tostadas are limited only by your imagination. I've listed my favorites. Use any or all as you desire.

CAMPECHE-STYLE SHRIMP
WITH GARLIC, CILANTRO, AND SOUR ORANGE JUICE

MAKES ENOUGH FOR 4 TOSTADAS

---

12 ounces (340 g) peeled, deveined shrimp (preferably wild)

1 clove garlic, peeled and minced

2 tablespoons chopped fresh cilantro

2 tablespoons sour orange juice (see Note) or fresh lime juice

2 teaspoons smoked or sweet paprika

Oil for the plancha

Coarse salt and freshly ground black pepper

Combine the shrimp, garlic, cilantro, sour orange juice, and paprika in a bowl and stir to mix. Marinate for 15 minutes. Heat your griddle or plancha to high and oil it well. Drain the shrimp well, then transfer to the hot plancha. Season with salt and pepper and cook until sizzling and browned, 2 minutes per side.

Assemble the tostadas with your garnish of choice.

Note: Sour orange (naranja agria) looks like a bumpy orange, with a decisively sour tang. You can approximate the flavor by using equal parts fresh orange juice and lime juice.

CHORIZO AND CARAMELIZED ONIONS

MAKES ENOUGH FOR 4 TOSTADAS

---

1 tablespoon extra virgin olive oil

1 small white onion, peeled and diced

12 ounces (340 g) raw chorizo (if in link form, slit the casings and squeeze out the meat)

Heat the griddle or plancha to medium-high and oil it well. Add the onions and cook, stirring with an offset spatula until lightly browned, 2 to 3 minutes. Add the chorizo and cook, chopping it with the side of spatula, until sizzling and browned, 3 to 4 minutes. Move it to the side of the griddle. Cook the tostadas in the residual chorizo fat and assemble and top as desired.

LOADED QUESADILLAS

MAKES 2 (CAN BE MULTIPLIED AS DESIRED)

The quesadilla was the first Mexican dish I learned to make (thanks, high school buddy John Oschrin), and it remains a Raichlen standby. It's often described as a Mexican grilled cheese sandwich—with tortillas standing in for the bread. In Mexico, sometimes quesadillas come deep-fried and sometimes grilled; the griddle produces a crust of perfect crispness with melty-gooey cheese inside.

---

4 large (8-inch/20 cm) flour tortillas

2 tablespoons melted unsalted butter, plus butter or oil for the griddle

6 ounces (170 g) pepper Jack, Jack, cheddar, or a Mexican melting cheese like Oaxaca or Chihuahua, thinly sliced or coarsely grated

1 jalapeño chile, thinly sliced

ANY OR ALL OF THE FOLLOWING FILLINGS:

8 pitted black olives, thinly sliced

1 scallion, trimmed, white and green parts thinly sliced

3 tablespoons minced fresh cilantro

4 ounces (115 g) shredded cooked chicken or diced cooked shrimp

---

1. Place 2 of the tortillas on a work surface and brush the tops with melted butter. Invert so the butter side is down. Arrange the cheese on top, followed by the jalapeño and any of the optional fillings. Top with the remaining tortillas and brush the tops with more butter.

2. Heat your griddle or plancha to medium-high and butter or oil it well.

3. Arrange the quesadillas on the griddle and cook until sizzling and browned on the bottom and the cheese starts to melt, 1 to 2 minutes. Using an offset spatula, carefully turn the quesadillas over and cook the other side the same way.

4. Transfer to a platter or plates. Cut into wedges (or not) and dig in.

WHAT ELSE Quesadillas can be made with flour or corn tortillas, with cheeses ranging from tangy Oaxaca or Chihuahua to Jack, pepper Jack, or cheddar. Some people make quesadillas with a single large flour tortilla folded in half; others go the sandwich route, as I do here.

WHAT'S MORE To make a Spanish quesadilla, use Manchego cheese, substitute piquillo peppers for the jalapeños, and add thinly sliced, dried Spanish chorizo or jamón serrano.

CHAPTER 6

MEAT

This book began with a steak—literally. One of those luscious A5 Wagyu steaks from Japan. A steak so extravagantly marbled, conventional grilling would have set it on fire. But cook it on a teppan (as the Japanese call a griddle) and it comes out to carnivorous perfection. The Spanish have the same idea when they cook their solomillo con foie (sirloin steak with foie gras) on a plancha. Likewise, Mexicans, when they prepare their iconic carne asada. In this chapter, meat hits hot metal.

A5 WAGYU STRIP STEAK

SERVES 2 (CAN BE MULTIPLIED AS DESIRED)

This is it. The recipe that inspired this book. The recipe that necessitated this book. Normally, when I cook a steak, I do so over live fire—ideally wood or wood-enhanced—to smoke the meat as well as cook it. But there's one steak you simply can't grill over live fire, and it happens to be one of the most esteemed and expensive steaks in the world: A5 Wagyu from Japan. Wagyu refers to a breed of Japanese cattle (the name literally means "Japanese cow")—prized for its high degree of innate intramuscular marbling. The steers with the most marbling are rated A1 to A5, with cuts from the latter being so extraordinarily well marbled that they have the appearance of white lace draped over a red tablecloth. And it's not just any fat, but fat that tastes buttery and luscious, like foie gras. The problem with all that fat is that it tends to catch fire when you cook it on a conventional grill. (It's a little like trying to grill butter.) Enter the teppan—the Japanese griddle. The hot metal sears the exterior of the steak—without erupting in flame. The following recipe contains only two ingredients: steak and salt. But the results are so extraordinary that diners will pay upward of 30 dollars an *ounce (30 g)*—that's one bite—at a good restaurant to try it. Note: Keep the steaks refrigerated until cooking.

Two 3- to 5-ounce (85 to 145 g) A5 Wagyu steaks from Japan (½ inch/1 cm is the ideal thickness), cold

Coarse salt (sea or kosher)

Freshly ground black pepper (optional—it is not typically on A5 Wagyu in Japan, but I like it)

---

1. Heat your griddle or plancha to high. There is no need to oil it.

2. Generously season the steaks on both sides with salt. Arrange the steaks on the hot griddle. Cook until sizzling, browned, and crusty on both sides, 2 to 4 minutes per side for medium. (Note: In Japan, A5 steaks are typically eaten medium, not rare.)

WHAT ELSE So where do you buy A5 Wagyu from Japan? When I started writing about barbecue, it simply wasn't available in the US. Now you can order it by mail though a half dozen quality meat purveyors who import it directly from Japan. The short list includes Crowd Cow, Holy Grail Steak Company, Snake River Farms, Meat N' Bone, and so on. As for the beef itself, like fine wine, much of it is associated with a single farm in Japan, such as Kagoshima Farms. A5 steak is extremely rich: 3 to 5 ounces (85 to 145 g)—about the size of a deck of playing cards—is considered a normal serving.

WHAT'S MORE An added advantage of cooking on a griddle: The steak fat will gather on the griddle, where you can use it to cook potatoes, rice, or bread. Try cooking the Smash Browns on page 209 or the fried rice on page 223 in Wagyu steak fat. Just saying.

GRIDDLED RIB EYES
WITH PEPPERONCINO CHIMICHURRI

SERVES 4

Steak with chimichurri is Argentina's national dish. The latter—a tart, pesto-like sauce made from parsley, garlic, olive oil, and vinegar—makes the perfect foil to the richness of the beef. In the following recipe, the steak gets a double blast of chimichurri flavor, first from a chimichurri dry rub, then from the classic sauce here enhanced with piquant pepperoncini.

FOR THE CHIMICHURRI RUB

1 tablespoon coarse salt
  (sea or kosher)

1 tablespoon freshly ground black
  pepper

1 tablespoon dried oregano

1 to 2 teaspoons hot red pepper flakes

1 teaspoon granulated garlic or
  garlic powder

FOR THE STEAKS AND FOR SERVING

4 rib eye steaks, each ½ to ¾ inch
  (1 to 2 cm) thick and 8 to 10 ounces
  (225 to 285 g), cold

Extra virgin olive oil for the griddle

4 whole pepperoncini

Pepperoncino Chimichurri (recipe follows)

YOU'LL ALSO NEED
A griddle dome (optional)

---

1. Make the chimichurri rub: Combine the salt, pepper, dried oregano, hot red pepper flakes, and granulated garlic in a small bowl and stir to mix. (Note: This makes more rub than you'll need for this recipe. Store any excess in a sealed jar away from heat and light—it will keep for several months.)

2. Generously season the steaks on both sides with the chimichurri rub. Drizzle on both sides with olive oil, patting the seasonings and oil into the meat with the flat of a fork.

3. Heat your griddle or plancha to high. Oil it well.

4. Arrange the steaks on the griddle and cook until sizzling and browned on the bottom and cooked to taste: 2 to 3 minutes per side for rare, 4 minutes per side for medium. If you're cooking on a cold night, cover the steaks with a griddle dome to hold in the heat.

5. Transfer the steaks to a platter or plates. Top each with a whole pepperoncini. Serve at once with the Pepperoncino Chimichurri spooned on top or on the side.

(recipe continues)

PEPPERONCINO CHIMICHURRI

MAKES ABOUT ¾ CUP (120 G)

Chimichurri (the sauce) traditionally contains four main ingredients: parsley for freshness, garlic for pungency, vinegar for acidity, and olive oil to bring it all together. (Additional flavorings might include oregano and hot red pepper flakes.) In this version, pepperoncini provide both piquancy and heat. For even more umami flavor, add a couple of chopped oil-cured anchovies.

---

2 or 3 cloves garlic, peeled and roughly chopped

1½ cups (90 g) packed fresh flat-leaf parsley leaves

5 pepperoncini, stems discarded, cut into ¼-inch (6 mm) slices

½ cup (120 ml) extra virgin olive oil

1 to 2 tablespoons red wine vinegar, or to taste

Coarse salt (sea or kosher—you'll need only a little) and freshly ground black pepper

---

Combine the garlic, parsley, and pepperoncini in a food processor and finely chop. Gradually work in the olive oil and vinegar. Add a little water if the sauce is too thick—it should be pourable. Add salt and pepper to taste: The mixture should be highly seasoned. The chimichurri tastes best within 4 hours of making.

SIRLOIN
WITH FOIE GRAS (SOLOMILLO CON FOIE)

SERVES 4

This meaty double-decker is a tapas bar classic in Spain, where steaks are often cooked on the plancha. This one comes topped with a crusty slab of seared foie gras. You'll love how the buttery duck liver enriches the beefy sirloin. For even more enrichment, serve the Sherry-Caramelized Onions on top by way of a sauce. A big thanks to Barbecue Bible 500 Club founders Robbie and Alynne Douglass for turning me onto this dish. American expats living in Spain, the Douglasses cooked every recipe (all 537) in *The Barbecue! Bible* cookbook during their COVID lockdown. They now help other grilling fanatics around the world achieve barbecue greatness! (Check out the Barbecue Bible 500 Facebook page.)

Extra virgin olive oil for the griddle

4 small sirloin steaks or filets mignons, each ¾ inch (2 cm) thick and 5 to 6 ounces (145 to 170 g)

4 slices of fresh foie gras, each ½ inch (1 cm) thick and 2 to 3 ounces (60 to 85 g)

Coarse salt (sea or kosher) and freshly ground black pepper

Sherry-Caramelized Onions (recipe follows; optional)

1 tablespoon minced fresh chives or flat-leaf parsley

---

1. Heat your griddle or plancha to high. Oil it well.

2. Generously season the steaks and foie gras on both sides with salt and pepper. Arrange the steaks on the griddle and sear until cooked to taste: 2 to 3 minutes per side for medium-rare. When the steaks are nearly done on the second side, arrange the foie gras slices on the griddle and sear until crusty and brown on both sides and just barely cooked through, 30 to 60 seconds per side. Don't overcook, or the foie gras will melt.

3. Transfer the steaks to a platter or plates. Top with the seared foie gras. Spoon the sherry-caramelized onions, if using, on top and dust with chopped chives or parsley.

(recipe continues)

WHAT ELSE You'll need to know about one special ingredient: foie gras—the incredibly rich, meltingly tender liver of specially raised ducks and geese. Look for it at high-end butcher shops. One good online source is dartagnan.com. You could substitute shiitake or portobello mushrooms for a different sort of umami taste. If you like your steaks flavorful, use sirloin. If you like your steaks fork-tender, use filet mignon.

WHAT'S MORE Some tapas bars serve the steaks on slices of buttered griddled bread (see page 120). For even sweeter caramelized onions, use a Spanish fortified wine called Malaga.

SHERRY-CARAMELIZED ONIONS

MAKES ½ TO ¾ CUP (80 TO 120 G)

---

3 tablespoons unsalted butter

1 sweet onion (like a Vidalia or Walla Walla), peeled and finely chopped

1 to 2 tablespoons sugar (less or no sugar if using Malaga wine)

1 cup (240 ml) cream sherry (or dry, but use more sugar) or Malaga wine

Coarse salt (sea or kosher) and freshly ground black pepper

---

1. Melt 2 tablespoons of the unsalted butter in a medium saucepan over medium-high heat. (You can place the pan on the griddle or plancha if you desire.) Add the onions and cook until a deep golden brown, stirring often. This will take 8 to 12 minutes, and as the onions brown, you'll need to lower the heat to keep them from burning. Once browned, stir in 1 tablespoon of the sugar, and cook until the sugar dissolves, 1 minute.

2. Add the sherry and increase the heat to high. Boil the sherry until the liquid is reduced to about ¼ cup (60 ml). Stir in the remaining 1 tablespoon butter and salt and pepper to taste. You want a thick but pourable mixture. Taste for sweetness, adding sugar as necessary. The onions should be sweet and sour. The caramelized onions can be prepared several hours ahead (store at room temperature) and reheated.

CARNE ASADA TACOS
(MEXICAN SEARED BEEF TACOS)

SERVES 4

Carne asada is to Mexico what the cheesesteak (page 81) is to Philadelphia. The preparation varies from region by region and street stall to street stall, but the basic elements include crisply griddled chopped steak piled on tortillas with chiles, scallions or onions, and salsa. Often, carne asada is grilled, but just as often it comes hot off the comal, as griddles are known in Mexico. Here's the basic script. Feel free to improvise.

1 pound (455 g) skirt steak, flap meat, or flank steak

Coarse salt (sea or kosher) and freshly ground black pepper

Garlic powder

Dried oregano

2 banana peppers, cubanelles, or jalapeños, or 1 poblano chile

1 bunch of scallions or 1 medium sweet onion, peeled

Canola or olive oil for the griddle

FOR SERVING

About 8 small (4-inch/10 cm) corn tortillas

Pico de Gallo (page 150) or other favorite salsa

Sour cream (optional)

Lime wedges

1. Season the steak on both sides with salt, pepper, garlic powder, and dried oregano. If using flank steak, cut it in half through the side before seasoning. (It helps to imagine the meat as a thin book lying on its back—the knife goes in through the edge of the pages, then you open the steak like a book.) Ideally, the thickness will be ¼ to ⅜ inch (6 to 10 mm).

2. Cut the peppers in half lengthwise and seed. Trim the roots off the scallions, or if using an onion, trim off the root end and cut the onion into 8 wedges.

3. Heat your griddle or plancha to medium-high with one zone on low for warming. Oil the griddle well.

(recipe continues)

4. Arrange the peppers and scallions or onion on the medium-high zone and griddle until browned on all sides and soft, turning with tongs, 3 to 6 minutes per side for the peppers, a little less for the scallions. Transfer the veggies to a cutting board. Cut the peppers lengthwise into ¼-inch (6 mm) strips. Cut the scallions into 2-inch (5 cm) lengths or, if using onions, roughly chop them. Return the veggies to the griddle and keep them warm on the low zone.

5. Increase the griddle heat under the medium-high zone to high.

6. Re-oil the griddle. Arrange the steak on top and cook until sizzling, browned, and cooked through, 2 to 3 minutes per side, turning with tongs. Transfer to a cutting board and thinly slice across the grain or cube it with a cleaver. Or move it to the low zone and slice it right on the griddle (use an old knife whose edge you don't mind blunting).

7. Arrange the tortillas on the griddle and cook until hot and pliable, 10 to 20 seconds.

8. To serve, transfer the tortillas to a platter or plates. Pile each with steak, peppers, and scallions or onions. Top with a spoonful of Pico de Gallo or other salsa. I wouldn't say no to a dollop of sour cream. Add a squeeze of lime and dig in.

WHAT ELSE Traditional steaks for carne asada include flank, skirt, and flap, but you can also use round or sirloin. The key is to slice and griddle it thin to minimize the length of the tough meat fibers. You could also go upscale with thinly sliced New York strip, rib eye, or tenderloin.

WHAT'S MORE You can also make carne asada with thinly sliced pork or poultry. (One popular version calls for cecina—pork or other meat marinated in a paste of ancho chiles, onions, and vinegar—you can find a recipe for it in my book *The Barbecue! Bible*.)

PICO DE GALLO

MAKES 2 CUPS (540 G)

The traditional condiment for carne asada tacos is pico de gallo ("rooster beak," literally)—tomato jalapeño salsa. When choosing tomatoes, preferably select ones that have never seen the inside of a refrigerator. Although not strictly traditional, some people like to add salt and pepper to taste. For a smoky pico de gallo, add minced canned chipotle chiles in addition to or in place of the jalapeños.

2 luscious ripe red tomatoes

1 or 2 jalapeño or serrano chiles, finely chopped (for milder pico, seed the chile first)

½ sweet white onion, finely diced (about ½ cup/65 g)

1 clove garlic, minced (optional)

½ cup (30 g) chopped fresh cilantro

½ teaspoon freshly and finely grated lime zest (optional)

3 tablespoons fresh lime juice, or to taste

Combine the tomatoes, chiles, onion, garlic (if using), cilantro, lime zest (if using), and lime juice in a medium bowl and gently toss to mix. It tastes best served within 2 hours of mixing; if you need to keep it longer, chop and combine the ingredients, but don't toss until the last minute.

PINCHOS MORUÑOS
(SPANISH PORK KEBABS)

MAKES 8 TO 10 KEBABS, SERVES 4

Pinchos moruños are a Spanish tapas bar classic, not to mention a window into a millennium of culinary history. Literally translated from the Spanish as "Moorish kebabs," they're a nod to the colonizing of Spain by the Moors, Muslims from North Africa, starting in 711 CE and lasting for nearly 800 years. The Moors revolutionized Iberian art and architecture, and they introduced such essential flavorings as saffron and rosewater, such mainstay Spanish ingredients as almonds and rice, and such classic dishes as gazpacho and albóndigas (meatballs). The one ingredient they didn't use was pork—proscribed by the Quran. That aspect of the dish would evolve after 1492, when the last Moorish army was defeated at Granada, restoring Spain to Christian rule. The Moorish legacy lives on in this dish pungent with garlic, fragrant with saffron and cumin, and sharp with a vivifying squeeze of lemon juice.

1½ to 2 pounds (680 to 910 g) boneless pork shoulder

1 large sweet onion

FOR THE RUB

1 tablespoon coarse salt (sea or kosher)

1 tablespoon freshly ground black pepper

1 tablespoon sweet paprika (preferably Spanish)

1 tablespoon dried oregano

2 teaspoons ground cumin

2 teaspoons granulated garlic

1 teaspoon hot red pepper flakes

½ teaspoon ground cinnamon

¼ teaspoon saffron threads, crumbled between your fingers

Extra virgin olive oil for the griddle and for serving

1 lemon, cut into wedges and seeded, for serving

YOU'LL ALSO NEED

A large aluminum foil pan or baking dish

8 to 10 bamboo skewers (8 inches/20 cm)

(recipe continues)

1. Cut the pork into ¾-inch (2 cm) cubes. Don't be afraid to include the fat—it adds flavor.

2. Peel the onion and remove the furry root end. Cut the onion in half widthwise and cut each half into 6 wedges. Break the wedges into individual segments. (Save the smaller pieces for stock or soups.)

3. Thread the pork onto skewers, placing a piece of onion between the cubes. Arrange the resulting kebabs in a foil pan or baking dish.

4. Make the rub: Combine the salt, pepper, paprika, oregano, cumin, granulated garlic, hot red pepper flakes, cinnamon, and saffron in a small bowl and mix well. (Note: This makes more rub than you'll need for this recipe. Store any excess in a sealed jar away from heat and light—it will keep for several weeks.)

5. Generously season the kebabs on all sides with the rub. Drizzle with olive oil, rolling the kebabs to coat them. Cover the kebabs in the pan and marinate in the refrigerator for at least 30 minutes or as long as 2 hours—the longer they marinate, the richer the flavor.

6. Heat your griddle or plancha to high. Generously oil it with olive oil.

7. Arrange the kebabs on the hot plancha. Cook until sizzling and browned on all sides, 2 to 3 minutes per side, turning with tongs. Serve the pinchos at once, with an additional drizzle of olive oil and lemon wedges for squeezing.

WHAT ELSE I like to use pork shoulder or shoulder steaks for these pinchos. These cuts have more fat than loin or tenderloin and make the pinchos more succulent. Of course, you can use a leaner cut if you desire. Note: The *ne plus ultra* of Spanish pork is Iberico, and you can now order it in the US from Campo Grande (eatcampogrande.com).

WHAT'S MORE This preparation is also excellent with lamb—a meat that hews more closely to its Moorish roots. Use boneless shoulder or leg. Lamb chops could be seasoned and griddled the same way.

Do you want a nontraditional sauce to go with the pinchos? Try the Onion Tomato "Salsa" on page 109 or the salsa brava on page 58.

BARBECUE FLAVOR PORK CHOPS

SERVES 4

The griddle will never take the place of a grill or smoker. But it can turn out a darn good pork chop fragrant with all the spice and smoke flavors we associate with true barbecue. The secret is a technique deployed by pit masters everywhere: layering flavors. In this case, we're seasoning the pork with a rub (see the simple recipe that follows), then a smoky butter baste, and finally, a sizzling smear of barbecue sauce.

FOR THE CHOPS AND RUB

4 pork chops (each ½ inch/1 cm thick), preferably bone-in

3 to 4 tablespoons Raichlen's Barbecue Rub (recipe follows) or your favorite rub

Extra virgin olive oil for the griddle

FOR THE SMOKE BUTTER

3 tablespoons unsalted butter

½ teaspoon liquid smoke

FOR BASTING AND SERVING

½ cup (120 ml) of South Carolina Mustard Sauce (recipe follows) or your favorite barbecue sauce, plus more for serving

YOU'LL ALSO NEED

A griddle dome

1. Generously season the pork chops on both sides with barbecue rub. Drizzle with oil, patting the spices and oil into the meat with the flat of a fork.

2. Heat your griddle or plancha to high. Oil it well.

3. While the griddle heats, make the smoke butter: Melt the butter in a small saucepan over medium-high heat. Then stir in the liquid smoke.

4. Arrange the pork chops on the hot metal and cook until sizzling and browned on the bottom, 2 to 4 minutes, a little longer if the chops are thicker than ½ inch (1 cm). Turn the chops over and spoon smoke butter over the chops to baste.

5. Continue cooking, basting once or twice more with the smoke butter, until the chops are sizzling, browned, and almost cooked through, 2 to 4 minutes more.

(recipe continues)

6. Re-oil the griddle. Brush the top of the chops with barbecue sauce and invert the chops onto the newly oiled section of the griddle. Griddle until the chops are sizzling and browned on the bottom, 1 minute. Brush the top side with sauce, invert, and cook the same way. Transfer the pork chops to a platter or plates. Pour any remaining smoke butter over them and serve at once.

WHAT ELSE To add even more smoke flavor, use one of the smoke-griddling techniques described on page 18. In a nutshell, you heat your griddle or plancha on a charcoal grill, adding wood chips to the embers to generate smoke. Simply cover the grill while griddling the pork: The woodsmoke will do the rest. Alternatively, you place a handful of hardwood chips on the hot plancha. Once they start smoking, add the pork chops and cover the chops and the chips with a griddle dome to hold in the smoke. Note: Liquid smoke has a bad rap among barbecue circles, but it is, indeed, made with real hardwood smoke. Just don't let anyone see the bottle. ☺

WHAT'S MORE To make barbecue flavor chicken, substitute skin-on chicken thighs or breasts for the pork chops. Lamb chops would be prepared the same way. The cooking times would be about the same in both cases.

RAICHLEN'S BARBECUE RUB

MAKES ¾ CUP (75 G)

I use this basic barbecue rub on all manner of meats, poultry, and seafood. You won't need all of it for these pork chops. Store any excess in a sealed jar away from heat and light. It will keep for several weeks.

---

3 tablespoons coarse salt (sea or kosher)

3 tablespoons freshly ground black pepper

3 tablespoons sweet or hot paprika

3 tablespoons brown sugar (light or dark—your choice)

Combine the ingredients in a mixing bowl and mix, breaking up any lumps in the sugar with your fingers.

(recipe continues)

SOUTH CAROLINA MUSTARD SAUCE

MAKES 1 CUP (240 ML)

In keeping with the Carolina roots of this dish, I suggest a simple mustard barbecue sauce.

⅓ cup (50 g) Dijon mustard

⅓ cup (50 g) brown sugar (light or dark—your choice)

⅓ cup (80 ml) apple cider vinegar

Garlic powder

Onion powder

Hot sauce

Coarse salt (sea or kosher) and freshly ground black pepper

Combine the mustard, brown sugar, and cider vinegar in a medium saucepan over medium-high heat. Add garlic powder, onion powder, hot sauce, and salt and pepper to taste. Gently simmer the sauce until thick and richly flavored, 5 minutes, whisking well. Store any excess in a sealed jar in the refrigerator, where it will keep for several weeks.

FIRE EATER LAMB CHOPS
(SPICED WITH CUMIN AND RED PEPPER IN THE STYLE OF WESTERN CHINA)

SERVES 4

China has many styles of barbecue, for example, the sweet-salty char siu ribs and pork tenderloins that have made their way to American Chinatown shops. Elsewhere, the pungency of cumin and the fiery bite of red pepper flavor a meat much prized by Central Asians: lamb. Four simple seasonings are all it takes to produce lamb chops that explode in your mouth with flavor. The sesame oil adds a haunting nutty note.

FOR THE RUB

1 tablespoon coarse salt (sea or kosher)

1 tablespoon freshly ground black pepper

1 tablespoon ground cumin

1 to 3 teaspoons hot red pepper flakes, ground cayenne pepper, Chinese chili powder, or gochugaru

2 pounds (910 g) lamb rib chops (12 to 16 ribs—ideally ½ to ¾ inches/ 1 to 2 cm thick)

2 tablespoons toasted sesame oil, plus more for the griddle

YOU'LL ALSO NEED

A griddle dome

1. Make the rub: Combine the salt, black pepper, cumin, and hot red pepper flakes in a small bowl and stir to mix. Add the red pepper flakes to suit your taste—the hotter, the better!

2. Brush the lamb chops with sesame oil on both sides and season with the rub on both sides, reserving 2 teaspoons rub for the end.

(recipe continues)

3. Heat your griddle or plancha to high, with one zone on medium. Oil the griddle with sesame oil.

4. Arrange the lamb chops on the high zone. Griddle until browned on both sides and cooked to taste, 2 to 4 minutes per side for medium, a little longer for medium-well, covering the chops with a griddle dome if desired to speed up the cooking. If the chops start to brown too much too fast, move them to the medium zone.

5. Sprinkle the chops with the reserved rub and serve at once.

WHAT ELSE There are several options for heat. You could use Chinese ground chiles or a chili powder blend known as la jiao mian. Alternatively, use Korean gochugaru, cayenne pepper, or hot red pepper flakes.

WHAT'S MORE I call for lamb rib chops here (which are easy to eat with your fingers). You can also use lamb loin chops (cook over medium-high heat for 3 to 5 minutes per side) or cubed lamb leg or shoulder threaded onto bamboo skewers to make kebabs. (Follow the cooking instructions in the Spanish pork kebabs, page 151.) For that matter, the preparation is pretty awesome on pork chops or kebabs. Follow the cooking instructions for Barbecue Flavor Pork Chops (page 153).

CHAPTER 7

POULTRY

Somewhere between the chicken spiedies (kebabs) served
at a Greek diner in upstate New York and the chicken teriyaki
dished up by a Japanese teppan yaki (steakhouse) master in
Tokyo, poultry discovered the griddle. The hot metal delivers
the results we've come to expect: crisp surface searing, rich
Maillard flavors, and remarkable ease of cooking. (Not only that,
but it's fast—faster than sautéing and roasting.) Whether you
crave the sophistication of seared duck breasts or chicken fingers
designed to bring out the child in all of us, the griddle will help
you do it better.

CHICKEN FINGERS
FOR GROWN-UPS

SERVES 4

Consider the chicken finger. A perfect morsel of crispness on the outside and moistness on the inside—made from the mildest tasting part of the chicken, the tender. The following recipe takes a page from the Austrian Wienerschnitzel playbook. Namely, dip the tender first in flour, then in eggs beaten with mustard (okay—the mustard isn't strictly traditional, but it boosts the flavor), and finally in breadcrumbs (in this case, panko) before sizzling it in butter on a hot plancha (requiring much less fat than the Viennese version in the process).

---

2 pounds (910 g) chicken tenders, sinews removed (see What Else)

Coarse salt (sea or kosher) and freshly ground black pepper

1 cup (125 g) flour

3 large eggs (preferably organic)

2 tablespoons Dijon mustard (optional)

1½ cups (120 g) panko breadcrumbs

3 tablespoons finely chopped fresh flat-leaf parsley or tarragon leaves (optional)

Extra virgin olive oil for the griddle

About 3 tablespoons cold unsalted butter in a chunk for the griddle

Lemon wedges, for serving

YOU'LL ALSO NEED

A griddle press (or cast-iron skillet)

3 small aluminum foil pans or shallow dishes

---

1. Place each chicken tender between two sheets of plastic wrap (or in a large resealable plastic bag) and gently pound to the thickness of about ¼ inch (6 mm) using the side of a cleaver, a scallopine pounder, or the bottom of a cast-iron skillet.

2. Generously season each pounded tender on both sides with salt and pepper.

3. Place the flour in a small foil pan or shallow dish. Crack the eggs into a second foil pan and add the mustard (if using). Beat until smooth with a fork. Place the panko in the third pan and stir in the parsley or tarragon (if using). Have the three pans on the side table next to your griddle or plancha.

4. Heat your griddle or plancha to medium-high and oil it well. Impale the butter on a fork and use half of it to grease the griddle.

5. Using forks or tongs, dip each tender first in the flour to coat both sides (shaking off the excess), then in the beaten egg, and finally in the panko, again, shaking off the excess. Once coated, transfer the tenders to the griddle.

6. Cook until the bottoms are crusty and browned, 2 to 4 minutes. Regrease the griddle with more butter. Turn the chicken tenders over and cook the other side the same way. You can place the griddle press on top if you like to speed up the cooking. Poke the tops of the tenders with your finger to check for doneness: The tenders should feel firm to the touch.

7. Serve at once with lemon wedges for squeezing.

WHAT ELSE We love chicken tenders because they're, well, tender. But one part is tough: the slender string-like tendon running the length of the tender. To remove it, place the tender tendon side down at the edge of a cutting board. Grab the exposed part of the white tendon with one hand. Gently run the blade of a sharp knife over the tendon and just under the meat. (Hold it parallel to the cutting board.) Work in a gentle sawing motion from one end to the other. The idea is to cut off the tendon, removing as little meat as possible.

This recipe calls for chicken tenders, but you could also use whole breasts, pounding them flat between two sheets of plastic wrap or in a resealable plastic bag in the style of Italian chicken Milanese. (This also works with veal scallopine.) Same buttery crust, same tender meat, but in a format that buries the plate.

WHAT'S MORE

- **For a simple sauce,** combine 3 tablespoons Dijon mustard and 1 tablespoon sriracha with ¾ cup (170 g) mayonnaise. Add an optional 1 tablespoon minced jalapeño chiles (fresh or pickled—your choice) and/or chopped fresh cilantro and whisk to mix.

- **For a simple salad to serve with the chicken fingers,** toss 1 bunch of washed, dried, stemmed arugula with 2 tablespoons each fresh lemon juice and extra virgin olive oil. Add salt and pepper to taste: It's that easy.

BRICK CHICKEN
WITH CRISPY HERBS AND TOMATO-OLIVE SALSA

SERVES 4

When it comes to the new standing griddles, smash burgers grab the headlines. True, cooking a burger under a weight produces delectably crisp edges (you can read all about it on page 92). But there's another protein that benefits from pressure: the commonplace chicken breast. Italians have a colorful name for it: pollo al mattone, "brick chicken." We'll use the, er, high-tech version—a griddle press—and the weight compresses the meat, rendering it crisp, moist, and tender. For seasoning, I call for the usual Italian suspects: garlic, rosemary, sage, hot pepper flakes, lemon, and olive oil. The crispy rosemary and sage make for great nibbling, and the Tomato-Olive Salsa amplifies the whole dish (make it a little ahead of time so its flavors can meld).

---

4 boneless chicken breasts, 6 to 8 ounces (170 to 225 g) each (see What Else)

6 large sprigs fresh rosemary

4 fresh sage leaves, plus 4 whole sprigs

Coarse salt (sea or kosher) and freshly cracked black peppercorns

1 tablespoon hot red pepper flakes, or to taste (depends on your tolerance for heat)

2 cloves garlic, peeled and minced

Extra virgin olive oil for the griddle

2 Meyer or regular lemons, 1 for squeezing, 1 cut into 4 wedges for serving

Tomato-Olive Salsa (recipe follows) for serving

YOU'LL ALSO NEED

A griddle press or 2 bricks (if using the latter, wrap them in aluminum foil, shiny side out)

An instant-read thermometer

---

1. Trim any tendons off the chicken breasts. (See instructions on page 163.) Strip the leaves off 2 rosemary sprigs and finely chop. Finely chop the 4 sage leaves.

2. Arrange the chicken breasts in a baking dish just large enough to hold them. Generously season each on both sides with salt, pepper, hot red pepper flakes, garlic, and the chopped

(recipe continues)

rosemary and sage. Drizzle each on both sides with olive oil and squeeze lemon juice over the breasts. Transfer to the refrigerator and let marinate for 30 to 60 minutes, turning once or twice.

3. Brush the remaining rosemary branches and sage sprigs with olive oil and season with salt and pepper.

4. If using bricks, wrap them with aluminum foil, shiny side out. Heat your griddle or plancha to medium-high. Oil it well with olive oil.

5. Drain the chicken breasts and discard the marinade. Arrange the breasts on the griddle and top with a griddle press or foil-wrapped brick. Cook until the bottoms are sizzling

and browned, 3 to 5 minutes. Turn the chicken breasts over and cook the other side the same way. Use an instant-read thermometer to check for doneness. (Insert it through the thick end of the chicken breast toward the center: You're looking for an internal temperature of 165°F/74°C.)

6. Meanwhile, arrange the rosemary branches and sage sprigs on the griddle. Cook until crisped and browned, 2 to 3 minutes per side.

7. Transfer the chicken breasts to a platter or plates. Top each with the crisp rosemary and sage. (Yes, the leaves are edible—nibble them off the stem.) Serve with the lemon wedges and Tomato-Olive Salsa on the side.

WHAT ELSE Most chicken breasts are sold boneless and skinless, but if you can find skin-on breasts, your chicken will be even more luscious. I call for "chicken breasts," which is how they're sold at most supermarkets, but actually, they are half breasts. You can certainly use a brick if you want to (wrap it in foil first), but a griddle press works just as well (see page 12).

TOMATO-OLIVE SALSA

MAKES 2 CUPS (480 G)

I serve brick chicken with what I like to call Tuscan salsa—a simple tomato salad spiked with olives, capers, and lemon. It goes great with all manner of griddled chicken, steak, pork chops, fish, etc.

2 cups (17 ounces/480 g) cherry tomatoes (ideally, a mix of red and yellow tomatoes)

⅓ cup (50 g) pitted Kalamata olives or black olives

1 scallion, trimmed, white and green parts thinly sliced

2 tablespoons brined capers, drained

½ teaspoon freshly and finely grated lemon zest

2 tablespoons fresh lemon juice, or to taste

3 tablespoons extra virgin olive oil, or to taste

Coarse salt (sea or kosher) and freshly ground black pepper

Cut the cherry tomatoes in half and transfer to a mixing bowl with the juices. Add the olives, scallion, capers, lemon zest and juice, and olive oil. Toss to mix, adding salt, pepper, and additional lemon juice as needed to taste. The salsa should be highly seasoned. It can be made up to 2 hours ahead of time and stored at room temperature.

KOREAN BARBECUE-INSPIRED CHICKEN THIGHS

SERVES 2 TO 4

When I wrote *The Barbecue! Bible*, few Americans had heard of Korean barbecue. These days, it's as omnipresent as K-pop and the *Squid Game*. These chicken thighs blast your taste buds with flavor—the funky heat of the gochujang (fermented chili paste) counterpointing the nutty fragrance of sesame oil. Add rice vinegar for piquancy and sugar for a sweet touch, and you have chicken that explodes off the plate with flavor. I like to serve it with the fried rice on page 223.

½ cup (110 g) gochujang sauce

2 tablespoons toasted sesame oil, plus 2 more tablespoons more for the griddle

2 tablespoons soy sauce

2 tablespoons mirin or sake

1 tablespoon sugar, or to taste

1 teaspoon freshly ground black pepper

½ teaspoon sea salt, or to taste

1 tablespoon freshly and finely grated peeled fresh ginger

2 cloves garlic, peeled and minced

1 scallion, trimmed, white part minced, green part thinly sliced and set aside for garnish

4 boneless chicken thighs, 6 to 8 ounces (170 to 225 g) each, skin-on if possible

1 tablespoon toasted sesame seeds

YOU'LL ALSO NEED

A large aluminum foil pan

1. Make the marinade: Combine the gochujang, 2 tablespoons sesame oil, the soy sauce, mirin, sugar, pepper, salt, ginger, garlic, and scallion whites in the aluminum foil pan. Stir to mix with a fork.

2. Open the chicken thighs so they lie flat. Add them to the marinade, turning to coat both sides. Marinate the chicken, covered, for 1 to 4 hours in the refrigerator (the longer the chicken is marinated, the richer the flavor), turning once or twice.

3. Heat your griddle or plancha with one zone on medium and another on high. Oil the medium zone well with half of the remaining sesame oil.

4. Lift the chicken thighs out of the marinade with tongs, holding them up over the pan so the marinade drains back into the pan. Arrange the thighs, skin side down, on the medium zone of the griddle and cook until sizzling and the skin or meat is browned, 4 to 6 minutes. If the skin starts to brown too quickly, turn down the heat.

5. Meanwhile, place the foil pan with the marinade on the high zone and boil the sauce until syrupy, 2 to 4 minutes. The sauce must come to a bubbling boil.

6. Re-oil the medium zone of the griddle with the remaining sesame oil, invert the chicken onto it, and continue cooking until the other side is sizzling and browned and the chicken is cooked through, 4 to 6 minutes more. The total cooking time will be 8 to 12 minutes, as needed. The chicken should be seared and crisp on the outside. If additional searing is needed, move it briefly to the high zone.

7. Transfer the chicken to a platter or plates. Pour the boiled marinade over it. Sprinkle with the scallion greens and sesame seeds.

WHAT ELSE You'll need to know about some special ingredients for this recipe—all of which can be found at well-stocked supermarkets or ordered online. Gochujang sauce is the pourable version of gochujang paste—Korean fermented chili paste—it's mildly spicy and loaded with rich, salty, umami flavors. You can use the latter, but thin it with a few tablespoons water. Dark sesame oil, pressed from toasted sesame seeds, is one of the defining flavors of Korean cuisine. Most boneless chicken thighs are sold skin off, but if you can find skin-on, your chicken will be all the more crisp and flavorful.

Chicken thighs offer a darker, richer, fattier meat than do mild-flavored breasts. But you can certainly use the latter if you prefer. (Extra points—and crispness—if you can find skin-on boneless breasts.) The marinade works equally well on other proteins, from skirt steak to pork chops to tofu.

SMOKY, CRISPY CHICKEN THIGHS
WITH ALABAMA WHITE BARBECUE SAUCE

SERVES 4 TO 6

As we have seen, griddles and planchas offer many culinary benefits. But the one thing they *can't* do is make barbecue. Or can they? What got me into writing this book was a technique I developed called smoke-griddling. (In a nutshell, you heat your griddle on a charcoal grill, adding wood chunks to the fire to generate smoke.) But can you actually *smoke* on a griddle? You can, and these crusty on the outside, moist and smoky on the inside chicken thighs—served with Alabama's vinegary, peppery white barbecue sauce— offer edible proof.

---

2 pounds (910 g) chicken thighs
  (preferably skin-on and bone-in)

Coarse salt (sea or kosher) and plenty
  of freshly ground black pepper

Vegetable oil or olive oil for the chicken
  and griddle

Alabama White Barbecue Sauce
  (recipe follows)

YOU'LL ALSO NEED

2 wood chunks or 1½ cups (135 g)
  hardwood chips, soaked
  (if griddling on a charcoal grill)
  or ¼ cup (23 g) hardwood chips,
  unsoaked, or hardwood sawdust
  or pellets if using a standing
  griddle

An instant-read thermometer

---

1. Generously season the chicken thighs on both sides with salt and pepper.

2. Set up your grill for indirect grilling and heat to medium. Have a few coals in the center under where you'll position the griddle or plancha. Add the griddle and oil it with vegetable oil.

3. Place the chicken thighs skin side up on the griddle. Add 2 wood chunks or chips to the fire. Close the grill lid. Adjust the vents to obtain a temperature of 350°F (175°C) degrees.

4. Smoke-griddle the chicken thighs until sizzling, browned, and cooked through. (The internal temperature will be 165°F/74°C on an instant-read meat thermometer.) Alternatively, make a slit in the underside of the thighs to make sure there's no red at the bone. Invert the chicken thighs toward the end of the cooking time to crisp and brown the skin. The total cooking time will be 30 to 40 minutes.

5. Transfer the chicken to a platter or plates and serve with the Alabama White Barbecue Sauce on the side.

WHAT ELSE If you do your griddling on a charcoal grill, smoking is easy. But if you're working on a standing, gas-fired griddle, you can still smoke the chicken. The secret lies in burning wood chips on the griddle and capturing the smoke under a griddle dome.

WHAT'S MORE To cook the chicken thighs on a gas-fired griddle: Heat your griddle with one medium zone and one high zone. Oil the medium zone. Place the wood chips on the high zone of the griddle. After a few minutes, they'll darken and start smoking. At this point, using a scraper or spatula, slide them to the medium zone. Arrange the chicken on the griddle, skin side down. Lower the griddle dome over the chicken and smoking wood chips. Cook until the chicken thighs are sizzling, crusty, and browned on both sides, 4 to 6 minutes per side. Finish with the skin side up. Test for doneness and serve as directed above.

ALABAMA WHITE BARBECUE SAUCE

MAKES 1 CUP (240 ML)

This tangy white condiment is one of the world's more unusual barbecue sauces. It originated at Big Bob Gibson's in Decatur, Alabama, where legend has it that the original Big Bob created it in the 1920s for a customer who disliked tomatoes. It sounds strange. It *is* strange, but it goes great with barbecued chicken. Note: The freshly grated horseradish and mustard are optional (they're not in the traditional recipe), but I like how they spice up the chicken.

⅔ cup (150 g) mayonnaise (preferably Hellmann's)

⅓ cup (80 ml) distilled white vinegar

2 tablespoons prepared white horseradish or freshly grated horseradish (optional)

2 teaspoons Dijon mustard (optional)

1 teaspoon freshly ground black pepper

½ teaspoon coarse salt (sea or kosher)

Combine all the ingredients in a mixing bowl and whisk until smooth.

SESAME SOY CHICKEN
IN THE STYLE OF A JAPANESE STEAKHOUSE

SERVES 4

Teri means "chicken" in Japanese and *yaki* means "roasted" or "grilled." Here's Japan's most beloved chicken dish reimagined on the griddle. Actually, it doesn't take much reimagining, for teriyaki is often prepared on a teppan, as tabletop griddles are known in Japan. The marinade has something for everyone: soy sauce for salt lovers, sugar for sweet tooths, sesame oil for a toasted nutty flavor, and ginger and garlic to punch up the aromatics. Get the griddle heat right and the marinade cooks to a sweet-salty caramel-like glaze.

1½ pounds (680 g) chicken breasts

½ cup (120 ml) soy sauce

¼ cup (35 g) brown sugar (light or dark—your choice)

3 tablespoons mirin (sweet rice wine) or sake

3 tablespoons toasted sesame oil, plus more for the griddle

1 teaspoon freshly ground black pepper

1-inch (3 cm) piece of fresh ginger, cut crosswise into ¼-inch (6 mm) slices, lightly crushed with the side of a cleaver

2 cloves garlic, peeled and lightly crushed with the side of a cleaver

2 scallions, trimmed, white part crushed with the side of a cleaver, green part thinly sliced for serving

YOU'LL ALSO NEED

A large aluminum foil pan

---

1. Trim any sinews off the chicken breasts (see box, page 163). Place each between two sheets of plastic wrap or in a resealable plastic bag and pound to a thickness of ½ inch (1 cm) with the side of a cleaver, a scallopine pounder, or the bottom of a heavy skillet. (Pounding speeds up and evens the cooking.) Place the breasts in the aluminum foil pan.

2. Make the marinade. Place the soy sauce, brown sugar, and mirin in a mixing bowl. Whisk until the sugar crystals dissolve. Whisk in the sesame oil, pepper, ginger, garlic, and scallion whites. Pour this mixture over the chicken breasts, turning to coat several times. Marinate, covered, in the refrigerator, for 1 to 4 hours (the longer the chicken is marinated, the richer the flavor). Turn the chicken a few times so it marinates evenly.

3. Heat your griddle or plancha to medium-high with one high zone. Oil the medium-high zone well with sesame oil.

4. Lift the chicken breasts out of the marinade with tongs, holding them up over the pan so the marinade drains back into the pan. Arrange the chicken on the medium-high zone and cook until sizzling and the meat on the bottom is browned, 3 to 5 minutes.

5. Meanwhile, place the foil pan with the marinade on the high zone and boil the sauce until syrupy, 2 to 4 minutes. (If you're feeling punctilious, fish out and discard the ginger, garlic, and scallion whites. I like a sauce with some bite, so I leave them in.) The sauce *must* come to a bubbling boil.

6. Re-oil the griddle. Turn the chicken breasts over and cook for 2 minutes. Dip the breasts in the boiling marinade. Continue cooking the chicken until sizzling and browned on the other side and the chicken is cooked through. (Continue to boil the marinade.) Dip the chicken one more time just before serving. The total cooking time will be 6 to 10 minutes in all, as needed.

7. Transfer the chicken breasts to a platter or plates. Pour the boiled marinade over them. Sprinkle with the scallion greens.

WHAT ELSE The Japanese often prepare teriyaki with chicken thighs, prizing the dark meat for its richness and flavor. Americans tend to prefer the mild white meat of the breast, which is what I call for here. In Japan, the chicken would be cut across the grain into finger-wide strips as it's cooking on the griddle.

WHAT'S MORE This teriyaki marinade and griddling technique are well suited to a wide range of proteins, from steaks and pork chops to tofu and seitan. All should be sliced to a thickness of ½ inch (1 cm) before cooking.

THE ART OF TEPPAN YAKI

The first thing you learn as a teppan yaki chef-in-training is that it's even harder than it looks.

The staccato drum routine with your utensils. The twirling of your spatula like a baton. Cooking a four-course meal for eight people on a searing hot stainless-steel tabletop. Keeping said tabletop well-oiled enough to prevent sticking and clean enough to eat off of (literally). Producing consistent results meal after meal, night after night, while breathing pepper fumes and oil smoke. Maintaining an entertaining patter while cooking for rude dinner guests who stare at their cell phones—or even talk on their cell phones—ignoring your carefully choreographed performance. No matter how long you train and how competently you cook—all I can say is, it isn't easy.

This I know because I recently completed Benihana's daylong Be the Chef cooking course in preparation for cooking dinner for my family. And despite the patient coaching of my trainer—an animated young chef from the Dominican Republic named Elvin Perez—I never did quite master the spatula twirling. But I did gain some new griddle skills, not to mention a newfound respect for the chefs at Benihana who make the art of teppan yaki seem like kid stuff.

Teppan is the Japanese word for griddle; *yaki* means roasted or grilled. Together they describe a style of tabletop cooking that simultaneously combines a communal cooking and dining experience with performance art.

I could tell you about my first teppan yaki experience in Tokyo, where I feasted on an A5 Wagyu steak that cost more than my first month's rent at my apartment in college. (You can experience it yourself—see page 140.) But the best place to start is at Benihana—that icon of the American restaurant circuit. The concept is simple: Guests sit around a tabletop grill, while a chef trained in the arts of cooking and entertainment prepares their meal in real time as they watch. The menu runs to Japanese staples: fried rice, griddled vegetables, shrimp, and chicken or steak, with higher priced variations including lobster, scallops, or tuna. Showmanship is an important part of the experience, and the first thing I learned was how to make an egg appear magically under an overturned bowl.

The first dish I learned to make was fried rice—a three-phase preparation that starts with scrambling that magic egg on the griddle. Extra points for scrambling the egg into the shape of a chicken—accompanied by the predictable sound effects. Next come aromatic vegetables (chopped onion, scallion, and carrot) sizzled on the griddle, followed by a slab of cooked white rice. Said rice gets a double blast of flavor: first from salt, pepper, and a generous dollop of "Japanese ice cream" (said with a wink)—Benihana's signature garlic soy butter. Using a chopping motion with your metal spatula and carving fork, you reduce the mixture to a pile of fluffy grains. Last comes a fillip of "Japanese Coca-Cola" (said with another wink—it's soy sauce) and more frenetic chopping and your fried rice is ready.

Normally, rice would come as an accompaniment, not as a starter, and the cynic in me wondered if this wasn't a way to fill up diners at the onset of the meal, so guests wouldn't mind the relatively small portions of shrimp and steak that follow. But the cynic had little room for speculation, for it was time to cook the vegetables and the onion volcano. The former consisted of broad slabs of zucchini sliced lengthwise and cooked with butter, soy sauce, and toasted sesame seeds (see page 216). It even involved a cool trick: Position your salt shaker on your spatula and pound the handle with your fist. That shoots the shaker high in the air where you can grab it (theoretically), eliciting gasps of admiration from your onlookers. Unless you drop it. Which doesn't make the zucchini any less tasty.

Teppan is the Japanese word for griddle; *yaki* means roasted or grilled. Together they describe a style of tabletop cooking that simultaneously combines a communal cooking and dining experience with performance art.

Onion slices receive similar flavorings, and I was even able to accommodate a special request for darkly caramelized onions from one guest—my wife. Of course, burning came easily to this teppan yaki chef-in-training.

The onion volcano serves more as a party trick than something you eat, but it never fails to delight. In a nutshell, you separate the layers of a thick onion slice, then pile them into a cone, leaving a small hole at the top. Into this hole you pour safflower oil, followed by vodka, then you touch a butane match to the top. If you do it right, fire whooshes up like a Roman candle, which my trainer slides along the griddle with his carving fork, making choo-choo sounds to simulate a train. (For my take on the dish, see page 219.)

Next comes the shrimp—served in two sizes, one as an appetizer, one as part of the main course, both ceremoniously butterflied and sectioned on the hot griddle. This enables you to unsheathe the chef's knife hanging menacingly at your side in a metal scabbard. The shrimp get seasoned with butter and lemon juice—the latter involving squeezing a lemon wedge with tongs and a fork without ever touching it with your fingers. In fact, nothing gets touched with your fingers—which certainly runs counter to the way I cook. Use your tools, not your hands, my trainer explained repeatedly. I'm not quite sure what purpose all the slicing and dicing of the shrimp served beyond showmanship—except to make it easier to eat with chopsticks.

The pièce de résistance was a strip steak, cut thin—as all food cooked on the teppan should be—with a thick finger of fat left at one end. My trainer showed me how to rub this finger of fat over the griddle to grease it (neat trick), then brown the steak in the beef fat. The cooking is quick—30 seconds per side suffices for medium-rare. More knife work reduces it to bite-size pieces, but whether that's to make it easier to chopstick, or make the meat seem more tender, I can't say.

What I can say, is that working with a simple palate of flavors—salt, pepper, and soy sauce here, sesame seeds, garlic butter, and fresh lemon juice there—Benihana chefs create a symphonic range of flavors. And with that, the chefs—yours truly included—take their bow. The kids breathe a sigh of relief: They can finally pull out their cell phones. My training ends with the presentation of a red diploma.

SPIEDIES

(GREEK AMERICAN CHICKEN KEBABS)

SERVES 4

Spiedies are chicken or beef kebabs popular in upstate New York. (The word comes from the Italian *spiedo*, meaning "sword" or "skewer"; the dish was popularized by Greek diner and food truck owners.) Tradition calls for flavoring the meat with bottled Italian dressing. My version takes the homemade route, combining olive oil (extra virgin), vinegar (red wine), garlic (fresh), and oregano to make Italian dressing from scratch.

FOR THE KEBABS

1½ pounds (680 g) boneless chicken breasts or thighs, preferably skin-on

2 green or red bell peppers, stemmed and seeded

1 small sweet onion

1 bunch fresh sage, stemmed

FOR THE MARINADE/SAUCE

½ teaspoon each coarse salt (sea or kosher) and freshly ground black pepper

2 teaspoons Dijon mustard

3 tablespoons red wine vinegar, or to taste

¾ cup (180 ml) extra virgin olive oil, plus more for the griddle

FOR SERVING

4 pita breads

Sliced tomatoes

Sliced lettuce

Pepperoncini or other hot peppers

YOU'LL ALSO NEED

8 bamboo skewers (8 inches/20 cm)

---

1. Cut the chicken into ¾-inch (2 cm) cubes. Cut the pepper into ¾-inch (2 cm) pieces. Cut the onion in half widthwise, peel it, then cut each half into 6 wedges. Separate the onion wedges into individual layers. (You'll use the larger pieces for assembling the kebab. Finely chop the smaller pieces to add to the marinade.)

2. Thread the chicken, pepper, large onion pieces, and sage leaves alternately onto bamboo skewers. Arrange the skewers in a baking dish.

(recipe continues)

3. Make the marinade/sauce. Combine the salt, pepper, and mustard in a mixing bowl and whisk to mix. Gradually whisk in the vinegar. Whisk in the oil in a thin stream: The mixture should emulsify (come together and thicken). Whisk in the chopped onion. Alternatively, whirl the marinade in a blender. Correct the seasoning, adding salt or vinegar to taste: The mixture should be highly seasoned.

4. Pour two-thirds of the marinade over the chicken skewers, rotating the latter a few times so they marinate evenly (set aside the remaining marinade for serving). Marinate in the refrigerator for at least 30 minutes, or as long as 4 hours, rotating the skewers a few times (the longer the chicken is marinated, the richer the flavor).

5. Just before serving, heat your griddle or plancha to high. Have one zone on medium. Oil the high zone well.

6. Drain the spiedies well, discarding the marinade. Arrange the skewers on the hot zone and cook until sizzling and browned on all sides, 1 to 2 minutes per side, 4 to 8 minutes in all.

7. Meanwhile, arrange the pitas on the medium zone of the griddle and cook until warm, 20 seconds per side, turning once.

8. To serve the spiedies, place 2 kebabs on a pita bread and fold the bread over them, using the bread to hold the kebabs in place while you pull out the skewers. Pile on tomato, lettuce, and pepperoncini if desired. Spoon a little of the reserved marinade/sauce over the meat and serve.

WHAT ELSE Chicken breasts are easier to cube, but chicken thighs give you more flavor. (Dark meat always does.) If you can buy it with skin on, so much the better. Note: The fresh sage leaves aren't traditional, but I like the way they pump up the flavor.

WHAT'S MORE Spiedies are often made with diced lamb or beef. For the former, use boneless shoulder or leg; for the latter, use sirloin or tri-tip. Some people serve their spiedies on the skewer, with the pita on the side. Others unskewer the spiedies on hoagie rolls, in which case I'd add a generous slather of mayonnaise first.

CRISPY SKIN DUCK BREASTS
WITH CHERRY HORSERADISH RELISH

SERVES 4

Think of a steak: the meat red and beefy, with a sizzling edge of fat that's as buttery crisp as a pork crackling. Now imagine that steak once had wings. That's pretty much how to describe a duck breast. Whole duck is time-consuming to prepare. Duck breast delivers these flavor dividends in minutes. And there's no better way to cook it than on the griddle. The hot metal sears the skin crackling crisp. The dark rich meat pairs well with fruit (think French duckling à l'orange). Here's the postmodern version, with a cherry horseradish relish you can make in less than 3 minutes.

FOR THE RELISH

¾ cup (170 g) cherry preserves

¼ cup (60 g) prepared or freshly grated horseradish, or to taste

½ teaspoon freshly and finely grated lemon zest

1 tablespoon fresh lemon juice, or to taste

¼ teaspoon ground cinnamon, or to taste

FOR THE DUCK BREASTS

4 duck breasts, each 7 to 8 ounces (200 to 225 g)

Sesame oil or extra virgin olive oil

Coarse salt (sea or kosher) and freshly ground black pepper

Ground cinnamon in a shaker jar

YOU'LL ALSO NEED

An instant-read thermometer

1. Make the cherry relish: Place the cherry preserves in a mixing bowl. Stir in the horseradish, lemon zest and juice, and cinnamon. Keep at room temperature until serving.

2. Using a sharp paring knife, trim any tendons off the duck breasts (see box, page 163). Score the skin on each breast in a diamond pattern, making the cuts ¼ inch (6 mm) apart, cutting toward, but not through, the duck meat.

(recipe continues)

3. Lightly brush or drizzle the duck breasts on both sides with oil. Season generously on both sides with salt, pepper, and a very light sprinkling of cinnamon.

4. Heat your griddle or plancha to medium in one zone and high in another.

5. Lightly oil the medium zone and arrange the duck breasts on top skin side down. Cook until the fat renders and the skin browns and crisps, 8 to 12 minutes. Take your time and lower the heat as needed: The crackling crisp skin is the best part of the duck.

6. Lightly oil the high zone and invert the duck breast onto it. Cook until the meat side is browned and the duck is cooked to taste—to an internal temperature of 135°F (57°C) for medium-rare; 145°F (63°C) for medium—1 to 2 minutes. (Use an instant-read thermometer inserted through the *side* of the duck breasts to check for doneness.)

7. Transfer the duck breasts to a platter or plates and serve with the cherry horseradish relish on the side.

WHAT ELSE It used to be that buying duck breasts required a trip to a specialty butcher. Today, you find them in the meat section of many supermarkets. One good online source is dartagnan.com. For convenience, I call for prepared horseradish, but if you take the time to grate fresh horseradish from scratch, your relish will be even more electrifying.

WHAT'S MORE As the skin crisps, a lot of duck fat will render onto your griddle. At my house, we fry brioche slices in the duck fat to serve with the duck. Or use it to cook the Plancha Potato Chips on page 204. Just saying.

CHAPTER 8

SEAFOOD

Quick: What's the most common fear people have about cooking fish? Actually, there are three: drying it out, having it stick to the grill or pan, or falling apart when you try to turn it. The griddle, with its even heat and smooth stick-resistant surface, eliminates all three. In this chapter, seafood hits the flattop, from a cutting-edge candied salmon (seared with brown sugar and maple syrup) to the Charm City crabcakes I grew up on. In France we find a traditional sole meunière and from Asia, sesame-seared tuna and teppan yaki shrimp. When it comes to seafood, fear no more.

SOLE MEUNIÈRE
WITH BROWN BUTTER

SERVES 4

For the last 25 years, I've promoted the virtues of grilling—going so far as to proclaim that if something tastes good baked, fried, or sautéed, it probably tastes even better grilled. Yet some foods just can't be grilled—among them fragile flatfish, like sole and flounder. The best way to cook these is lightly dusted with flour prior to searing them on hot metal—a preparation the French call *à la meunière* (literally, "in the style of the miller's wife"). Enter your griddle, which keeps the fish moist and crusty—without leaving half of it stuck to the grill grate. And an outdoor griddle keeps any potential spattering or fish smells out of your kitchen. Admittedly, a recipe whose primary ingredients consist of flour, salt, and pepper may sound simpleminded, but this is one of the tastiest and easiest ways I know to prepare fish.

---

8 tablespoons (1 stick/115 g) unsalted butter

1 cup (125 g) all-purpose flour

1 tablespoon sweet, hot, or smoked paprika (optional)

1 teaspoon freshly and finely grated lemon zest (optional)

2 pounds (910 g) fillet of sole or flounder

Coarse salt (sea or kosher) and freshly ground black pepper

2 tablespoons minced fresh flat-leaf parsley or chives

Lemon wedges, for serving

YOU'LL ALSO NEED
A griddle dome
A shallow dish or aluminum foil pan

---

1. Heat your griddle or plancha to medium-high.

2. Place the butter in a small skillet on the stove or on the griddle (if using the latter, have one zone on high) and cook until it starts to brown, swirling the pan so it browns evenly: First it will melt, then it will sizzle (as the water in the butter evaporates), and finally, it will start to turn brown as the milk solids in the butter begin to caramelize. This will take about 3 minutes in all. Remove the pan from the heat.

3. Meanwhile, place the flour in a shallow dish. Stir in the paprika and/or lemon zest, if using.

4. Season the fish on both sides with salt and pepper. Using tongs, dip each fillet in flour to coat both sides, gently shaking the fish over the pan to release any excess flour.

5. Using a spoon or silicone brush, spoon or brush some of the brown butter on the griddle. Arrange the fish on top. Cook until crusty and browned on the bottom, 2 to 4 minutes, depending on the thickness of the fillets. Butter another section of the griddle and invert the fish on top of it, using an offset spatula. Cook the other side the same way. To speed up the cooking or if the fillets are really thick, cover with a griddle dome. To check for doneness, press a fillet in the thickest part with your finger. It will break into clean flakes when cooked through.

6. Transfer the fish to a warm platter or plates and pour the remaining brown butter over it. Sprinkle with chopped parsley or chives. Serve with lemon wedges.

WHAT ELSE There are many options for sole, depending on where you live. Here in New England, where I spend much of the year, we find lemon sole, grey sole, and flounder. On the West Coast, you might find petrale sole. Or if you're feeling bucks up, you might buy the most refined flatfish of all: Dover sole imported from Europe. But any delicate fish fillet can be cooked with this method. Note: The classic recipe contains only salt, pepper, and flour, but sometimes I jazz up the flour with paprika (sweet, hot, or smoked) and freshly grated lemon or lime zest.

WHAT'S MORE For Cajun-style sole meunière, add a tablespoon or two of Cajun or Creole seasoning to the flour and omit the salt (unless you're using a salt-free variety) and the pepper. For American Southern-style fish, substitute fine cornmeal for the flour (this preparation works well for catfish). For extra flavor, add 2 tablespoons of drained capers to the melted butter, letting them crisp up as it browns.

CANDIED SALMON
(CRUSTED WITH BROWN SUGAR, MAPLE SYRUP, AND MUSTARD)

SERVES 4

Candied salmon is a staple of the smokehouses of the Pacific Northwest—not to mention one of our perennially popular blog posts on Barbecuebible .com. This sweet, crusty fish will make believers even out of people who don't normally like salmon. The secret: Paint the fish with Dijon mustard, then dredge it in brown sugar, and sear it on a hot griddle. The sugar caramelizes, producing a candy-sweet crust, keeping the fish moist in the center. Note: It's important to salt the salmon with an assertive hand to counterpoint the sweetness.

---

2 pounds (910 g) skinless salmon fillets, each cut on the diagonal into 4 equal pieces

Coarse salt (sea or kosher) and freshly ground black pepper

½ cup (110 g) Dijon mustard

1 cup (145 g) brown sugar (light or dark—your choice)

3 tablespoons cold unsalted butter in a chunk for the griddle

¼ cup (60 ml) pure maple syrup

YOU'LL ALSO NEED

Needle-nose pliers or kitchen tweezers

A griddle dome

An instant-read thermometer (optional)

---

1. Heat your griddle or plancha to medium-high.

2. Run your fingers over the salmon fillets, feeling for pin bones. Remove any you find with needle-nose pliers or kitchen tweezers. Season the fish generously, and I mean generously, on both sides with salt and pepper. Paint the fish with the mustard on both sides.

3. Spread out the brown sugar in a baking dish, breaking up any lumps with a fork. Dredge the salmon on both sides in the brown sugar.

4. Impale the chunk of butter on a fork and rub half of it over a section of the griddle just large enough to accommodate the salmon. When the

(recipe continues)

butter is melted and sizzling, arrange the salmon on top. Cover with a griddle dome. Cook until crusty and browned on the bottom, 2 to 3 minutes.

5. Grease another section of the griddle with the remaining butter. Using a spatula, invert the salmon and brown the other side the same way 2 to 3 minutes; a minute longer per side for fully cooked. Note: Some of the sugar may burn and the fish may stick a little. That's normal. Just pry it up with your spatula. To check for doneness, press the top of the fish with your finger. It should break into clean flakes and look slightly pink in the center.

6. Transfer the salmon to a platter or plates and drizzle with the maple syrup. Serve at once.

WHAT ELSE I like to prepare this dish with wild king salmon. King because it's the fattiest and most luscious of the five varieties of salmon we eat in North America, wild because it has a better texture and flavor than farmed salmon. Alternatively, you could use sockeye or coho salmon, but they won't come out quite as moist. To add an extra dimension of flavor, you could smoke-griddle the salmon, following the instructions on page 18. The fried rice on page 223 makes a great accompaniment.

WHAT'S MORE Candied salmon is super quick and easy to make (it requires only a handful of ingredients), but it will leave your griddle rather messy. Thorough buttering helps reduce the sticking, and your metal grill spatula will help you remove any excess burnt-on sugar. If that fails, pour on hot water, bring it to a boil on the griddle, and use a metal scrubber, such as a Chore Boy, to scour it.

SESAME SEARED TUNA
WITH WASABI CREAM SAUCE

SERVES 4 TO 6

Who first had the brilliant idea to crust flash-seared tuna with sesame seeds? Regardless of the provenance, it was love at first sight and first bite. We loved the nutty crust and the speckling (which came from the use of both black and white sesame seeds). We loved the quick meaty char on the outside of the fish, the center still sushi rare. And nothing cooks it better than a hot griddle or plancha. Serve with soy sauce piqued with wasabi, as you would sashimi, or with the Wasabi Cream Sauce that follows. Note: While experimenting with this recipe, I crusted some of the tuna with cracked black peppercorns. Think of it as tuna au poivre. In the following recipe, I combine the sesame seeds with pepper, but you can certainly use only one or the other.

⅓ cup (80 ml) soy sauce

¼ cup (60 ml) toasted sesame oil, plus more for the griddle

¼ cup (60 ml) mirin (sweet rice wine) or sake

2 pounds (910 g) tuna in thick (ideally 1½-inch/4 cm) steaks or even thicker (2-inch/5 cm) loins

1 cup (110 g) sesame seeds (white or a mix of white and black)

¼ cup (30 g) cracked black peppercorns (or more sesame seeds)

Wasabi Cream Sauce (recipe follows) or soy sauce and wasabi paste for serving

YOU'LL ALSO NEED

A large aluminum foil pan

A shallow dish

---

1. Trim the tuna, if necessary, to remove any silver skin or sinew.

2. Combine the soy sauce, sesame oil, and mirin in the aluminum foil pan and whisk to mix. Add the tuna. Marinate, covered, in the refrigerator for at least 1 hour or as long as 4 hours (the longer it marinates, the richer the flavor). Turn several times so the tuna marinates evenly.

3. Heat your griddle or plancha to medium-high with one zone on high. Oil the medium-high zone well with sesame oil.

4. Spread the sesame seeds and/or cracked peppercorns in a shallow dish. Lift the tuna out of the marinade with tongs and let it drain. Dip each piece of fish in the sesame seeds and/or cracked

(recipe continues)

peppercorns, turning it to coat all sides. Shake off the excess.

5. Place the foil pan with the marinade over the high zone. Bring to a boil and reduce until syrupy. You'll use this as a sauce for the tuna.

6. Arrange the tuna on the medium-high zone. Cook until the sesame seeds are toasted and the outside of the tuna is cooked (the center should stay raw),

30 to 60 seconds per side or as needed, gently turning with your spatula or tongs.

7. Transfer the tuna to a cutting board. Cut it from top to bottom into ¼-inch-wide (6 mm) slices. Fan these out and transfer them to a platter. Drizzle with the reduced marinade. Serve the Wasabi Cream Sauce or a wasabi and soy sauce mixture alongside for dipping.

WHAT'S ELSE If you live on the East Coast, you'll probably buy your tuna in steak form. These give you crimson, ribbon-like slices. If you live on the West Coast, you can likely find tuna loins—shaped like square-sided logs. Cut crosswise, loins give you postage stamp–shaped slices that are perfect for eating with chopsticks. Note: Mirin is Japanese sweet rice wine. If unavailable, substitute sake and add 1 tablespoon sugar or maple syrup to the marinade.

WHAT'S MORE Many fish can be given the sesame crust treatment, from almaco to snapper. Lower the griddle heat to medium. Unlike the tuna, you'll want to cook these fish all the way through.

WASABI CREAM SAUCE

MAKES ABOUT 1 CUP (225 G)

1 tablespoon wasabi powder

1 cup (225 g) mayonnaise
(preferably Hellmann's)

1 tablespoon soy sauce, or to taste

Combine the wasabi powder with an equal amount of warm water in a small mixing bowl. Stir into a paste and let stand for 2 minutes. Whisk in the mayonnaise and soy sauce. Note: This probably makes more sauce than you need. Any leftover will keep for several days in the refrigerator.

A NEW FISH SANDWICH
(AKA SNAPPER MILANESE)

SERVES 4

Some years ago, dining at a Daniel Boulud restaurant, my wife and I experienced an extraordinarily crisp snapper fillet. The chef had cut paper-thin slices of country-style white bread on a meat slicer, then used them to crust the fish. It was a twist on traditional Milanese (thin protein crusted with flour, egg, and breadcrumbs), and its buttery crunch and supernaturally moist fish left us awestruck. Most of us don't have a meat slicer at home, but you can achieve a similar effect with commercial thin-sliced bread, such as Pepperidge Farm, or Argentinean pan de miga.

1½ pounds (680 g) boneless, skinless snapper or other delicate white fish fillets

Coarse salt (sea or kosher) and freshly ground black pepper

8 slices of thin-sliced bread, crusts removed (save them for breadcrumbs)

3 tablespoons unsalted butter at room temperature, plus 3 tablespoons cold unsalted butter in a chunk for the griddle (or as needed)

Lemon wedges, for serving

YOU'LL ALSO NEED
A griddle dome

---

1. Generously season the fish on both sides with salt and pepper.

2. Place 4 slices of the bread on a baking sheet. Lightly spread the top of each slice with half the room-temperature butter and invert. Arrange the fish on top and top with the remaining bread slices. Spread the remaining room-temperature butter on top.

(recipe continues)

3. Meanwhile, heat your griddle or plancha to medium. Cut the cold butter in half, impale 1 piece on a fork, and rub it across the griddle in an area just large enough to accommodate the sandwiches.

4. When the butter is melted and sizzling, arrange the fish sandwiches on top. Cover with a griddle dome. (If your dome is too small, you may need to work in 2 batches.) Cook the sandwiches until the bottoms are crisp and a dark golden brown, 3 to 5 minutes.

5. Slide the sandwiches to another section of the griddle. Impale the remaining cold butter on the fork and use it to grease the griddle again. Use a spatula to carefully invert the sandwiches on top of the melted butter. Cover again with the griddle dome. Continue griddling until the bread on the bottom is crisp and darkly browned and the fish is cooked through, 3 to 5 minutes more.

6. Serve at once, with lemon wedges for squeezing.

WHAT ELSE You want a quick-cooking fish for this recipe. Here in Miami, I use snapper. Other good choices would include black bass, flounder, sand dabs, and sole. For a more traditional coating for the fish, use the breadcrumb coating in Chicken Fingers for Grown-ups (page 162).

WHAT'S MORE A guilty conscience is a terrible thing. When I finished the sandwich chapter in this book, I realized I forgot to include a recipe for a Reuben sandwich. Basically, it involves the same technique as the fish sandwich here. So . . . substitute thin-sliced rye bread for the white bread. Sandwich it with thinly sliced corned beef (or pastrami), a few tablespoons of sauerkraut (drained well), and sliced Emmentaler or other Swiss cheese. Cook it on the griddle until the bread is toasted and browned and the cheese is melted, 3 to 5 minutes per side. As with the fish sandwich, cover with a griddle dome to hold in the heat.

TEPPAN YAKI SHRIMP

SERVES 4

You've seen it at Benihana and other Japanese steakhouses: griddled shrimp with garlic soy butter—the perfect fusion of briny umami flavors with the nutty crunch of sesame seeds. The preparation takes mere minutes; the results are out of this world. And, no, you don't need to flip the shrimp tails into your shirt pocket the way your favorite hibachi chef does. The fried rice on page 223 makes a great accompaniment.

FOR THE GARLIC SOY BUTTER

1 to 2 cloves garlic, peeled

8 tablespoons (1 stick/115 g) unsalted butter, in a bowl at room temperature

1 to 2 tablespoons soy sauce

FOR THE SHRIMP

Canola or olive oil for the griddle

2 pounds (910 g) shrimp, preferably large and wild, peeled and deveined (leave the tails on)

Fresh white or black peppercorns in a peppercorn grinder

2 tablespoons toasted sesame seeds

2 tablespoons thinly sliced scallion greens

1. Make the garlic soy butter. Using a Microplane, grate the garlic over the butter. (Alternatively, use a garlic press or smash and then mince the garlic with a chef's knife.) Add the soy sauce to taste and stir or whisk until thoroughly mixed. (This makes more garlic soy butter than you need for this batch of shrimp. Store any excess, covered, in the refrigerator, or roll it into a cylinder in a sheet of plastic wrap and store it in the freezer.)

2. Just before serving, heat your griddle, teppan, or plancha to medium-high. Oil it well. Add the shrimp and top with freshly ground pepper and a generous spoonful of the garlic soy butter. Griddle until the shrimp are lightly browned and cooked through, 2 to 3 minutes per side, depending on the size of the shrimp. Add additional butter to taste. Note: Benihana chefs make a ceremony of cutting the shrimp into pieces on the griddle. This speeds up the cooking time. I don't usually bother.

3. Just before serving, sprinkle the shrimp with the sesame seeds and scallion greens.

(recipe continues)

WHAT ELSE Garlic soy butter is easy to make—provided you remember to have the butter at room temperature. It's great not just for shrimp and other shellfish, but for chicken, mushrooms, and fried rice. I always keep a cylinder of it wrapped in plastic wrap or parchment paper on hand in the freezer. It keeps for up to three months and is great sliced on steaks.

WHAT'S MORE Both the shrimp and butter are infinitely customizable. For a Thai-inspired take, for example, substitute fish sauce for the soy sauce and add finely grated lime zest, lime juice, and a little sugar. For a Spanish twist, add pimentón (smoked paprika) and minced scallion greens to the butter.

SCALLOPS
WITH MARCONA ALMOND PICADA

SERVES 4

"The flamenco guitars, the jacaranda trees, the raisin-y aroma of Oloroso sherry aging in dark cellars," write my expat friends Robbie and Alynne Douglass. "Jerez is the heart of Spain's Sherry Triangle and it isn't easily forgotten." The Douglasses moved from California to the south of Spain just prior to COVID. They spent their lockdown cooking every recipe in my book *The Barbecue! Bible*. Thus prepared, they launched the Barbecue Bible 500 Club for other people wishing to cook their way through the book (check out the Facebook page). And they regularly regale me with recipes from their adopted homeland. Case in point: these scallops seared on the plancha and topped with picada—a sherry, almond, and breadcrumb mixture that heightens the scallop flavor without overpowering it.

FOR THE PICADA

2 tablespoons extra virgin olive oil, preferably Spanish, plus more for the griddle

2 cloves garlic, peeled and thinly sliced

¼ cup (30 g) Marcona almonds, ground to fine crumbs (not a paste) in a food processor

¾ cup (30 g) fresh breadcrumbs (preferably homemade from country-style white bread)

¼ cup (15 g) chopped fresh cilantro or flat-leaf parsley

1 teaspoon freshly and finely grated lemon zest

2 tablespoons fresh lemon juice, or to taste

1 tablespoon sherry (preferably Oloroso)

½ teaspoon sherry vinegar, or to taste (optional)

Salt (sea or kosher) and freshly ground black pepper

FOR THE SCALLOPS

16 large sea scallops (1½ to 2 pounds/ 680 to 910 g total)

¾ cup (95 g) all-purpose flour

1. Prepare the picada: Place 2 tablespoons of the olive oil in a medium skillet over medium-high heat. Add the garlic and ground almonds and cook until fragrant, 1 minute. Add the breadcrumbs and cook until the mixture is lightly browned, 2 minutes, stirring often.

(recipe continues)

Stir in 2 tablespoons of the cilantro, the lemon zest and juice, the sherry, and sherry vinegar (if using). Add salt and pepper to taste: The mixture should be highly seasoned. (The picada can be made several hours ahead; let it cool and store it in a bowl in the refrigerator. Rewarm it before serving; see Step 4.)

2. Just before serving, rinse the scallops under cold water and pat dry with a paper towel. Season them with salt and pepper. Place the flour in a shallow pan or bowl.

3. Heat your griddle or plancha to medium-high with one zone on medium. Oil the medium-high zone well.

4. Place the picada in a skillet (or an aluminum foil pan) on the medium zone of the griddle and heat it through, stirring occasionally.

5. Meanwhile, dip the top and bottom of each scallop in flour, shaking off the excess. Arrange the scallops on the medium-high zone of the griddle. Cook, turning once, until browned on both sides and just barely cooked in the center, 1 to 2 minutes per side.

6. Transfer the scallops to a warm platter or plates. Spoon the hot picada over the scallops. Sprinkle with the remaining cilantro and serve.

WHAT ELSE You'll need to know about a few special ingredients for this recipe—all readily available online or at a well-stocked supermarket. Marconas are nearly round Spanish almonds with an elegant nutty flavor (they're widely available these days, including at Whole Foods and Trader Joe's). American almonds will get you in the ballpark. You could also use skinned hazelnuts. Oloroso (literally "scented") refers to dry or semidry sherry. The preparation goes equally well with fish fillets or shrimp.

CHARM CITY CRABCAKES

MAKES 4 CRABCAKES, SERVES 4 AS AN APPETIZER, OR 2 AS AN ENTRÉE

The crabcake is one of the glories of American gastronomy—especially in the city where I grew up, Baltimore. So why are there so many bad renditions masquerading as the real McCoy? The offenses are many: inferior crab, unnecessary fillers, distracting flavorings like onions and peppers. Well, I'm here to tell you how to make a proper crabcake and how to cook it on your griddle. First the crab: Start with fresh jumbo lump. Yeah, it's expensive, but I promise you it's worth the splurge. Next, the binder. In my hometown we use mayonnaise, egg, and cracker crumbs. (Sometimes we use white bread soaked in half-and-half and wrung out—I'll tell you how to do it; see What's More.) Finally, the flavorings. Actually, there are only two: dry mustard and Old Bay seasoning. Keep the alliums (onion and garlic) and capsicums (bell and hot peppers) out of it. As for the griddle, it solves two potential problems posed by the traditional way of cooking crabcakes in Maryland: deep-frying and broiling. The former adds unwanted fat. With the latter, it's often hard to cook the crabcake through without burning the exterior.

---

1 pound (455 g) jumbo lump crab meat

1 large egg (preferably organic)

⅓ cup (75 g) mayonnaise (preferably Hellmann's)

2 teaspoons Old Bay seasoning, or to taste

1 teaspoon dry mustard

¼ cup (20 g) cracker crumbs

2 to 3 tablespoons cold unsalted butter in a chunk for the griddle

Extra virgin olive oil (optional)

Made-from-Scratch Tartar Sauce (recipe follows), for serving

YOU'LL ALSO NEED
A griddle dome

---

1. Gently pick through the crab, removing any pieces of shell.

2. In a large mixing bowl, beat the egg with a fork or whisk until smooth. Stir in the mayonnaise, Old Bay seasoning, and dry mustard. Add the crab and sprinkle the cracker crumbs on top. Fold as gently as possible with a rubber spatula just to mix. (Or use your hands to mix.)

(recipe continues)

3. Line a plate with plastic wrap. Dampen your hands and divide the crab mixture into four equal portions. Form each one into a patty about ¾ inch (2 cm) thick and place on the lined plate. You can cook the crabcakes right away, but they'll hold together better if you chill them, covered with plastic wrap, for 30 minutes.

4. Heat your griddle or plancha to medium-high. Impale the butter chunk on a fork and use it to grease the griddle.

5. Gently arrange the crabcakes on the buttered griddle. Cook until sizzling and browned on both sides and cooked through, 2 to 4 minutes per side or as needed, using an offset spatula to turn once. If your crabcakes are really thick, cover with a griddle dome to speed up the cooking. If the crabcakes start to stick, add more butter or squirt the griddle with a little olive oil. Serve at once with the Made-from-Scratch Tartar Sauce on top.

WHAT ELSE For the ultimate crabcake, use fresh jumbo lump crabmeat from Maryland. It doesn't come cheap, but it's worth it. Check with your local fishmonger (alternatively, two good mail order sources are Cameronsseafood .com and Crabplace.com). If you live on the West Coast, you can make awesome crabcakes with Dungeness crab.

WHAT'S MORE Some people use a panade (cream-soaked bread) as a binder in place of the cracker crumbs and maintain that it produces a lighter, moister crabcake. Dice 1 slice of white bread (remove the crusts) and place it in a bowl with ¼ cup (60 ml) half-and-half. Soak for 5 minutes. Drain off the half-and-half, gently wringing the bread through your fingers.

MADE-FROM-SCRATCH TARTAR SAUCE

MAKES 1 CUP (225 G)

Having gone to all the time and expense of making your crabcakes from scratch, for heaven's sake, don't use a sugary bottled tartar sauce. Here's how to make this classic condiment from scratch.

¾ cup (170 g) mayonnaise (preferably Hellmann's)

1 tablespoon Dijon mustard

1 tablespoon brined capers, drained

1 tablespoon minced cornichons or dill pickle

1 tablespoon minced fresh chives or scallion greens

1 tablespoon chopped fresh tarragon or basil

½ teaspoon freshly and finely grated lemon zest

2 teaspoons fresh lemon juice

Freshly ground black pepper

Place the ingredients in a bowl and whisk to mix, adding lemon juice to taste. Any leftovers will keep, covered, in the refrigerator for at least 3 days.

CHAPTER 9

VEGETABLES, RICE & TOFU

Vegetables may not be the first food you think of for the griddle. A Japanese yaki master would beg to differ. The Japanese cook everything from asparagus to mushrooms to zucchini on a hot teppan (griddle), and the dry searing heat enhances the natural sweetness of each one. If griddles are great for breakfast pancakes, they're also great for zucchini pancakes and potato latkes. The flat, stick-resistant surface works equally well for smashing potatoes, frying rice, and yes, fragile foods like tofu.

PLANCHA POTATO CHIPS

SERVES 2 TO 4

Potato chips are such an integral part of American packaged snack foods, it's hard to remember that chefs once took pride in frying them fresh. (A few—too few—still do.) And you may be surprised to learn that most commercial potato chips are made with dried potato flakes, cornstarch, and water—formed into a pasta-like dough, stamped out on a machine, and fried in oil. Ouch. Which makes these plancha potato chips all the more remarkable because they actually deliver the rich, earthy taste of fresh potatoes. Another advantage: They're cooked with a fraction of the fat, and it's a great-tasting fat—extra virgin olive oil. Plancha potato chips are a staple at our house, and I hope they will become one at yours.

---

2 large baking potatoes, or 4 medium
    Yukon Golds, peeled

Extra virgin olive oil for the griddle

Coarse salt (sea or kosher) and
    freshly ground black pepper

YOU'LL ALSO NEED
A wire cooling rack

---

1. Cut the potatoes crosswise into ⅛-inch-thick (3 mm) slices, using a mandoline or a steady hand with a chef's knife. Spread the potato slices out on a clean dish cloth or paper towels and blot dry with additional paper towels. Work quickly so the potatoes don't oxidize.

2. Meanwhile, heat your griddle or plancha to medium-high. Oil it well.

3. Arrange the potato slices in a single layer on the griddle. Season them with salt and pepper and cook until sizzling and browned on the bottom, 2 to 4 minutes. Lightly drizzle the tops with oil, then turn with tongs, season, and cook the potato slices on the other side the same way.

4. If you like your potato chips extra crispy, transfer them to a wire rack over a sheet pan. They'll crisp upon cooling. We like them hot, so we serve them hot off the plancha.

WHAT ELSE I've made these chips from all manner of potatoes, from Idaho bakers to Yukon Golds. You can even make them with sweet potatoes—which, because they're harder and drier, are a little more difficult to slice. Practically speaking, the larger the potatoes, the fewer you need to slice, cook, and turn. To facilitate slicing, use a mandoline: I like my Japanese model made by Benriner, available at kitchenware stores or online.

WHAT'S MORE Myriad are the seasonings you can put on plancha potato chips. I'm partial to barbecue rub, smoked paprika, Old Bay seasoning, and Cajun seasoning.

Cooking enthusiast and reader of my books David Wright wrote me about a sandwich his father used to make when he was growing up during the lean years of World War II: "We'd fry potato slices, then pile them on fresh buns with mayo, ketchup, mustard, pickles, sliced onions, sliced tomatoes, and cheese. You didn't even miss the hamburgers, and I never had anyone not ask for seconds." Amen!

LATKES

(JEWISH POTATO PANCAKES)

MAKES ABOUT SIXTEEN 3-INCH (8 CM) LATKES, SERVES 4 TO 6

Like most health-conscious Americans, I generally try to avoid eating excess fat. But there's one holiday that positively revels in fat—the Jewish Festival of Lights, better known as Hanukkah. The holiday celebrates the victory of a small band of Hebrew freedom fighters known as the Maccabees over an occupying Greek army in 164 BCE. When the Jews went to rededicate the temple, they found only enough oil to kindle the sacred candelabra for one night. Miraculously, this oil burned for eight nights, and ever since, Jews have celebrated Hanukkah by eating foods fried in oil. Which brings us to these crusty potato pancakes, redolent with onion and traditionally served with sour cream and applesauce. In my BG (Before Griddle) days, I cooked them in a frying pan, but that required multiple batches (not to mention an exceedingly messy stove). A standing griddle can handle enough latkes for a whole Hanukkah party and takes the mess outside.

1½ pounds (680 g) russet or Yukon Gold potatoes, peeled

1 small to medium onion, peeled

¼ cup (30 g) flour or matzo meal

1 teaspoon baking powder (optional)

2 large eggs (preferably organic), lightly beaten with a fork

¼ cup (15 g) finely chopped fresh flat-leaf parsley

1 teaspoon coarse salt (sea or kosher), plus more as needed

½ teaspoon freshly ground black pepper, plus more as needed

Canola or olive oil for the griddle

Sour cream for serving

Applesauce for serving

YOU'LL ALSO NEED

A food processor fitted with a course shredding disk or a box grater

Cheesecloth (optional)

---

1. Coarsely grate the potatoes and onions in a food processor fitted with a shredding disk or on a box grater. (Work quickly.) Grab handfuls of the grated vegetables and squeeze tightly between your fingers to wring out as much liquid as possible. To wring the liquid out even more efficiently, wrap the grated vegetables in cheesecloth and twist hard.

(recipe continues)

2. Transfer the grated vegetables to a mixing bowl and stir in the flour and baking powder, followed by the eggs, parsley, and salt and pepper. (The latkes should be highly seasoned—you may wish to add more salt or pepper after tasting your first cooked latke.)

3. Meanwhile, heat your griddle or plancha to medium-high. Oil it well.

4. Spoon a small mound of the potato mixture onto the griddle to form a 2½-inch (6 cm) pancake. Fry until sizzling, crusty, and brown on both sides,

turning with a spatula, 2 to 4 minutes, or as needed. Transfer to paper towels to drain, then taste it—if it needs more seasoning, add some salt and pepper to the mixture. Spoon out the remaining mixture in batches, leaving 1 inch (3 cm) between latkes, and cook and drain as directed. Add additional oil as needed to keep the latkes from sticking.

5. Serve the latkes at once. Sour cream and/or applesauce are the traditional accompaniments.

WHAT ELSE Russets are the traditional potato for latkes, but I also like the creamy richness of Yukon Golds. If you make these latkes during Passover, use matzo meal instead of flour and omit the baking powder (the latkes may be a bit denser but still delicious).

WHAT'S MORE

- **To make smoked latkes** (yes, there really is such a thing), heat a plancha on a charcoal grill (see page 18). Add hardwood chips or chunks to the fire. When you see lots of smoke, oil the griddle well and spoon out the latke mixture on top. Cook the latkes as directed above. (Lower your grill lid to trap the smoke.)

- **To make sweet potato latkes,** substitute sweet potatoes for the Yukon Golds. They won't shed as much water when you wring them out. Cook them over medium heat, as they burn more easily than latkes made with white potatoes.

- **To make latkes with smoked salmon:** Prepare the latkes as directed above. Top each with thin slices of smoked salmon, a dollop of sour cream, and a sprig of fresh dill.

SMASH BROWNS
(AKA SMASHED POTATOES)

MAKES 8 SMASH BROWNS, SERVES 4 TO 6

Cross a baked spud with a latke (potato pancake—see page 206) and you get a smash brown. Buttery and crusty on the outside, creamy and soft inside, the smashed potato has taken the food world by storm. Most recipes start with small fingerling potatoes, which are great, but full-size potatoes give you a skin side and flesh side in a most appealing combination. My potato of choice is the Yukon Gold, with its creamy texture and buttery, earthy-sweet taste.

---

4 Yukon Gold potatoes or golden potatoes, scrubbed but with skin left on

3 tablespoons cold unsalted butter in a chunk for the griddle

Coarse salt (sea or kosher) and freshly ground black pepper

2 tablespoons finely chopped fresh chives (optional), for serving

YOU'LL ALSO NEED

A griddle press (or cast-iron skillet)

A griddle dome

---

1. Cook the potatoes by roasting or boiling (see What Else) until tender enough to pierce with a bamboo skewer. Roasting will take 45 minutes to 1 hour; boiling, 20 to 25 minutes. This step can be done up to 48 hours ahead. Cut each potato in half widthwise.

2. Heat your griddle or plancha to medium-high.

3. Impale the chunk of butter on a fork and use it to grease 8 circles on the griddle (each circle should be 1 inch/3 cm larger than the diameter of the potato halves). Arrange the potatoes, cut side down, on the butter. Cook until the bottoms are sizzling and browned, 3 to 5 minutes. Swab the tops of the potato halves with butter.

(recipe continues)

4. Using a griddle press or heavy weight (like the bottom of a small cast-iron skillet or saucepan), press down on the potatoes to smash them to a thickness of ¼ to ½ inch (6 mm to 1 cm). Rebutter the griddle as directed and turn the flattened potatoes over. Continue cooking the potatoes until sizzling and browned on the other side (the skin side), 3 to 5 minutes more. While the potatoes cook, season them with salt and pepper on both sides.

5. Transfer the smashed potatoes to a platter or plates. Sprinkle with chopped chives (if using) and dig in.

WHAT ELSE To make a smashed potato, you need to cook it first, and while it's possible to roast a whole potato on a griddle (cook it over medium heat under a griddle dome, turning often, for 30 to 40 minutes—it's ready when pierced easily with a wooden skewer), I usually boil the potatoes in salted water until tender or bake them in the oven or toaster oven at 400°F (200°C) for 45 to 60 minutes. Or smoke-griddle them (see page 18). Note: I call for butter for cooking the smash browns, but if you have duck fat or bacon fat, the flavor will be even richer. For extra flavor, you could cook a quartered shallot or two or a small onion alongside the potatoes.

WHAT'S MORE Fingerling and baby potatoes make great smash browns. Leave the skins on and scrub well. Boil in lightly salted water until tender when pierced with a skewer, 5 to 10 minutes. Prepare as directed above.

You can also smash sweet potatoes in this manner. If using baby sweet potatoes, cook, griddle, smash, and brown as directed above. If using medium sweet potatoes, cut them in half lengthwise, cook, griddle, smash, and brown as directed above. If using large sweet potatoes, cut them crosswise into 2-inch-thick (5 cm) rounds. Boil, smash, and griddle these cut side down until sizzling and browned on the bottom, 3 to 5 minutes, then turn and repeat on the other side. Add butter as necessary. Serve the smashed sweet potatoes drizzled with maple syrup or sprinkled with cinnamon sugar. Or why not—with both!

And for a smash brown with an Asian twist? Prepare the recipe above, substituting toasted sesame oil for the butter. Once smashed, brush the potatoes with sesame oil on both sides and dredge on both sides in 1 cup (110 g) sesame seeds in a shallow bowl. Continue griddling until the sesame seeds are golden brown.

Finally, by way of a topping, I recommend sour cream or Greek yogurt. Don't rule out grated Parmigiano-Reggiano and/or crumbled bacon.

ZUCCHINI PANCAKES
WITH SERRANO AND MINT

MAKES 12 PANCAKES, SERVES 3 OR 4 AS AN APPETIZER OR SIDE DISH, 2 AS A LIGHT MAIN COURSE

Zucchini has two great virtues—affordability and abundance. Zucchini has two drawbacks—a soft texture and a mild (dare I say bland) flavor. These simple pancakes take advantage of the former and remedy the latter. The secret: panko breadcrumbs for crispness and fresh mint and serrano chiles to pump up the taste. Sometimes I add a tablespoon of poppy seeds for extra color and crunch. By way of a sauce, I suggest a simple Minted Yogurt inspired by Greek tzatziki.

2 large eggs (preferably organic)

1 pound (455 g) zucchini, washed and trimmed

2 scallions, trimmed, white and green parts thinly sliced

3 tablespoons thinly slivered fresh mint (or 2 teaspoons dried)

1 serrano chile, seeded and minced (for spicier pancakes, leave the seeds in)

¼ cup panko breadcrumbs (or as needed to form a thick batter)

1 tablespoon poppy seeds (optional)

½ teaspoon finely grated lemon zest (optional)

Coarse salt (sea or kosher) and freshly ground black pepper

2 tablespoons cold unsalted butter in a chunk for the griddle

Extra virgin olive oil (optional)

Minted Yogurt (recipe follows; optional) for serving

YOU'LL ALSO NEED

A food processor fitted with a coarse shredding disk or a box grater

1. Beat the eggs in a large mixing bowl. Coarsely grate in the zucchini, using a box grater or the coarse shredding disk of a food processor. Add the scallions, mint, and serrano, then sprinkle on the panko and poppy seeds and lemon zest (if using). Add salt and pepper on top (start with ½ teaspoon of each, adding more to taste if needed after you've cooked the first pancake). Gently stir just to mix. You'll want to cook the pancakes right away—before the zucchini has time to go soggy.

(recipe continues)

2. Meanwhile, heat your griddle or plancha to medium-high.

3. Impale the chunk of butter on a fork and rub it over the plancha where you plan to cook the pancakes. Spoon blobs of the zucchini mixture onto the griddle to form 3-inch (8 cm) pancakes, leaving 1 inch (3 cm) between them. Gently flatten with the back of a spoon.

Cook the pancakes until sizzling and browned on both sides, turning with a spatula, 3 to 4 minutes per side. Add more butter or olive oil as needed to keep the griddle greased so the pancakes don't stick.

4. Transfer the pancakes to warmed plates or a platter and serve at once with the Minted Yogurt, if using.

WHAT ELSE Smaller zucchini tend to have a little more snap to them than the monsters. And don't let a lack of panko (Japanese breadcrumbs) stop you from making these pancakes. In a pinch, use conventional toasted breadcrumbs.

WHAT'S MORE These pancakes can be made with any summer squash, from yellow to pattypans to crooknecks.

MINTED YOGURT

MAKES 1 CUP (225 G)

1 cup (225 g) plain Greek-style yogurt
1 scallion, trimmed and minced
3 tablespoons thinly slivered fresh mint

1 lemon wedge for squeezing
Coarse salt (sea or kosher) and freshly ground black pepper

Place the yogurt in a mixing bowl. Whisk in the scallion, mint, a squeeze of fresh lemon juice, and salt and pepper to taste. Use immediately or store in the refrigerator for up to 4 hours.

ACORN SQUASH
WITH BACON AND MAPLE SYRUP

SERVES 2 TO 4

Here's a recipe so simple, it requires only three ingredients: bacon, squash, and maple syrup. But the interplay of flavors and textures—sweet, salty, smoky, soft, creamy, and crisp—is so compelling, I had to include it in this book. It looks cool—never underestimate the importance of looking cool at your griddle—and it's one of those versatile dishes you can serve as a pass-around, appetizer, or vegetable side dish.

---

1 large acorn squash

12 ounces (10 to 12 strips/340 g) bacon (see What Else)

Oil or butter for the griddle

Maple syrup for drizzling

YOU'LL ALSO NEED
A griddle dome (optional)

---

1. Cut the squash crosswise into ½-inch-thick (1 cm) rings. Use a spoon to scrape out the seeds (you can toast them for a snack—see What's More).

2. Holding a strip of bacon at both ends, gently stretch it, then wrap it around a squash ring. (You may need to use multiple strips.) Continue wrapping until all the squash rings are used up. You'll cook the top and bottom of the squash by themselves.

3. Heat your griddle or plancha to medium. Lightly oil the griddle and arrange the squash rings on top.

4. Griddle the squash rings until the bacon is crisp and browned on both sides and the squash is soft and cooked, 6 to 8 minutes per side. You may wish to place a griddle dome on top to speed up the cooking.

5. Once the bacon fat starts to render, place the squash top and bottom on the griddle. Cook these until browned and soft.

6. Transfer the squash to a platter or plates and drizzle with maple syrup. See, I told you it was easy.

(recipe continues)

WHAT ELSE As a rule, I like my bacon thick-sliced. (Almost all real smokehouse bacons come thick-sliced.) But thin slices are easier to use for wrapping. If you have thick slices, place them between two sheets of parchment paper and roll them out with a rolling pin to flatten.

WHAT'S MORE This squash was inspired by a dish that rocked the blogosphere a few years ago: grilled bacon-wrapped onion rings. (There's a great recipe for them in my book *Project Fire*.) These are even easier to prepare on the griddle, with less risk of fiery flare-ups.

As for the squash seeds, pull off the pulp and wash them well. Boil in salted water until soft, 5 to 10 minutes. Drain the squash seeds and blot them dry, then place them in a medium bowl. Toss with extra virgin olive oil and salt and pepper. Heat your griddle or plancha to medium. Arrange the squash seeds on top and cook until crisp and golden brown, 5 to 10 minutes, stirring and turning occasionally with a spatula. Transfer to a bowl. Let cool before eating. The squash seeds will keep for several days in a sealed container at room temperature.

TEPPAN YAKI ZUCCHINI

SERVES 2 TO 4

Zucchini is the vegetable many of us love to hate. All too often it comes to the table watery and bland. One great way to cook it is Japanese teppan yaki–style: Sear it on a screaming hot griddle with butter, soy sauce, and sesame seeds. I learned the technique during my brief stint as a Benihana chef (more about that on page 174). The hot griddle lays on a crusty sear, while the soy sauce and sesame seeds pump up the flavor.

---

2 zucchini (each about 8 inches/20 cm long)

2 tablespoons unsalted butter or toasted sesame oil

1 tablespoon soy sauce (in a food-safe squeeze bottle), or to taste

2 tablespoons sesame seeds

---

1. Cut the zucchini lengthwise into ¼-inch-thick (6 mm) strips.

2. Heat your griddle or teppan to high. Lightly grease it with the butter or sesame oil, using the flat of your spatula to spread it out in a thin film.

3. Arrange the zucchini on top and cook until sizzling and browned on the bottom, 2 to 3 minutes. Add butter or oil as needed so the zucchini doesn't stick. Sprinkle the zucchini with half of the soy sauce and sesame seeds.

4. Invert the zucchini with a spatula, sprinkle with the remaining soy sauce and sesame seeds, and cook the other side the same way. Serve at once.

WHAT ELSE This preparation works great for any high-moisture content vegetable, from sliced onions and mushrooms to eggplant.

WHAT'S MORE For the best results, use smallish zucchini (8 inches/20 cm or so in length) and slice them lengthwise. That gives you fewer pieces to manage and turn than if you slice the zucchini crosswise into rounds.

TORPEDO ONIONS
WITH TOASTED ALMONDS AND BALSAMIC GLAZE

SERVES 2 OR 3 (CAN BE MULTIPLIED AS DESIRED)

You've seen them at your local farmers market: slender, elongated onions with purplish bulbs and dark green shoots. Their mild onion-leek flavor makes them as delectable to eat as they are handsome to look at. The hot griddle caramelizes the natural plant sugars, making the onions smoky-sweet and cooking the outer sections to wafer crispness. I like serving torpedo onions with sweet, sour balsamic glaze and toasted almonds, but the truth is, they're pretty tasty with nothing more than salt and pepper.

---

1 bunch torpedo onions (6 to 8 onions)

2 tablespoons slivered almonds or pine nuts

2 tablespoons cold unsalted butter in a chunk for the griddle

Coarse salt (sea or kosher) and freshly ground black pepper

1 tablespoon balsamic glaze (see What Else)

---

1. Trim the green tops off the onions, leaving 1 inch (3 cm) of green closest to the bulb. (Save the onion greens for soups or stocks.) Cut each onion in half lengthwise, leaving the furry root end in place. (This helps hold the onions together.)

2. Heat your griddle or plancha to medium-high.

3. Place the almonds or pine nuts on the griddle and toast until fragrant and browned, 2 minutes, turning with a metal spatula or scraper. Transfer the nuts to a small bowl and let cool.

4. Impale the butter chunk on a fork and use it to rub half the butter on the griddle to grease it. Arrange the onion halves, cut side down, on top. Cook until sizzling and browned, 2 to 4 minutes.

5. Slide a metal spatula under the onions and lift. Grease the griddle with the remaining butter, then invert the onions on top and cook until the rounded sides (now on the bottom) are sizzling and browned, 2 to 4 minutes more. Season the tops of the onions with salt and pepper.

6. Transfer the onions to a platter or plates. Drizzle with the balsamic glaze and sprinkle with the toasted nuts. Delectable hot or at room temperature.

(recipe continues)

WHAT ELSE Torpedo onions are in season from late winter through summer. Balsamic glaze is a syrupy sweet-sour condiment made with balsamic vinegar and sugar or honey. Look for it online or at a high-end supermarket. For a Middle Eastern twist, substitute pomegranate molasses for the balsamic glaze.

WHAT'S MORE This technique can be used for all sorts of onions and alliums, from Vidalias to leeks. Here is the basic procedure for round onions: Heat your griddle or plancha to medium-high. Cut an onion, peeled, crosswise into ¼-inch-thick (6 mm) slices. Run a toothpick or two through the side of each slice to hold it together during griddling. Brush the onion rounds on both sides with some olive oil and season with salt and pepper. Grease the griddle and arrange the onion slices on top. Cook until sizzling and browned on the bottom, 2 to 4 minutes. Invert and cook the other side the same way. Shallots would be griddled using the same method. Peel and cut them lengthwise in quarters or halves. Remember to remove the toothpicks before serving.

ONION VOLCANO

SERVES 2 TO 4

The onion volcano is the ultimate griddle party trick—a signature at the Benihana restaurant chain, where, oddly, it's prepared but not served. In a nutshell, you build a cone-shaped pile of raw onion rings and fill the cavity with safflower oil and vodka. Touch a match to the top and flames shoot forth, just like an erupting volcano. Well, I've made an onion volcano—at Benihana no less (see page 175)—and I've rejiggered the recipe to give it more flavor. Note: As always with flambéeing, use a butane match or long safety match. Roll up your sleeves. Tie back your hair. Don your Kevlar vest (just kidding, but do be careful). You know the drill.

---

1 large perfectly round white onion, peeled

1 teaspoon safflower or other vegetable oil, plus oil in a squeeze bottle for the griddle

4 tablespoons (60 ml) cognac, brandy, whisky, or vodka

2 tablespoons unsalted butter, or as needed

2 tablespoons sesame seeds

1 tablespoon soy sauce, or to taste

YOU'LL ALSO NEED

2 long wooden matches or a butane match

Carving fork or kitchen tweezers

---

1. Cut the onion crosswise into clean, even, ¼-inch-thick (6 mm) slices. You'll use the third slice from the top for the volcano. (This slice will have sharply curved sides—perfect for forming the volcano.) Set the remaining slices aside for subsequent griddling.

2. Heat your griddle or teppan to medium-high, with one zone on medium-low. Oil it well, spreading the oil with the flat of your spatula.

3. Place the onion slice with the curved sides in the center of the medium-high zone. Arrange the remaining onion slices on the medium-low zone.

4. Using the edge of your spatula and your carving fork or a pair of kitchen tweezers, separate the onion slice with the rounded edge into individual rings. Carefully place the second largest ring atop the first, then the third largest, and so on, to form a volcano-shaped cone with a small hole at the top.

(recipe continues)

5. Squirt 1 teaspoon of the oil into this hole, then add 2 tablespoons cognac or other spirit (it helps to have them in a small pitcher, so you can pour the spirits in at once without having to fumble with measuring spoons). Immediately, touch the lit match or butane match to the top: Flames will start to shoot out, burn for a minute or so, then die out. And there's your onion volcano. Take a bow, then move the volcano to the cooler part of the griddle while you cook the remaining onion.

6. Melt 1 tablespoon of butter on the griddle (or squirt more oil) on the medium-high zone. Slide the remaining onion slices over to the medium-high zone. Deconstruct the onion volcano and add those rings as well. Griddle until the onions are golden brown on the bottom, 3 minutes. Turn the onions over and brown the other side the same way, adding more butter (or oil) as needed.

7. Cut each onion slice in half and cut each half in half again. Stir the onion with your carving fork or spatula to separate it into bite-size pieces. Add the sesame seeds and remaining 1 tablespoon butter, and cook for 1 minute. Add the soy sauce and continue cooking until the onions are darkly caramelized, 2 to 4 minutes per side. Pour on the remaining cognac and flambé it by touching a long match to it. Serve at once.

WHAT ELSE The secret to an onion volcano lies in the choice and cut of the onion. You need a perfectly round white onion. For fuel, Benihana uses vodka. You could use a spirit with more flavor: cognac or brandy. Cheers!

WHAT'S MORE The high drama of the onion volcano leads one to wonder what other vegetables could be ignited (but please—use caution!). Pattypan squash comes to mind. (Hollow it with a paring knife, cutting a small hole in the top.) Ditto small acorn squash sliced crosswise.

FRIED RICE AND COMPANY

SERVES 2 AS A MAIN COURSE, 4 AS A SIDE DISH

Call it grain's second coming. Call it the ultimate comfort food—served hot off the teppan (griddle) at your favorite Japanese steakhouse. Fried rice turns leftovers into the main attraction, and if those steakhouse chefs can amp it into performance art, just imagine what you can do when you when you fire up *your* griddle. Note: For the best results, use cooked rice that's a day or two old. Feel free to improvise.

Vegetable oil or toasted sesame oil for the griddle or teppan

1 large egg (preferably organic), lightly beaten in a small bowl with a fork

2 scallions, white part minced, green part thinly slivered on the diagonal and reserved

2 teaspoons minced peeled fresh ginger

1 clove garlic, peeled and minced

**FOR THE VEGETABLES
(ANY OR ALL OF THE FOLLOWING)**

1 small sweet onion, cut into ¼-inch (6 mm) dice

1 carrot, peeled, trimmed, and cut into ¼-inch (6 mm) dice

1 stalk celery, washed and cut into ¼-inch (6 mm) dice

4 ounces (115 g) green beans, strung and cut crosswise into ¼-inch (6 mm) pieces

½ cup (60 g) cooked or frozen peas

¼ cup (65 g) water chestnuts, cut into ¼-inch (6 mm) dice

FOR THE PROTEINS (OPTIONAL)

½ cup (120 g) diced tofu (see page 225)

½ cup (85 g) shelled shrimp, each cut in half crosswise

FOR THE RICE

3 to 4 cups (555 to 745 g) day-old cooked rice

1 to 2 tablespoons soy sauce, to taste

2 tablespoons unsalted butter, cut into chunks

Coarse salt (sea or kosher) and white or black pepper

---

1. Heat your griddle, teppan, or plancha to medium-high with one zone on low. Oil the griddle well.

2. Pour the egg onto the hot part of the griddle and scramble it, stirring and cutting with the side of your spatula. Move the scrambled egg to the cooler part of the griddle.

(recipe continues)

3. Re-oil the griddle. Add the scallion whites, ginger, and garlic to the griddle and fry until fragrant and lightly browned, 1 to 2 minutes, stirring with the side of the spatula.

4. Add the vegetables of your choice plus all but 1 tablespoon of the scallion greens (reserve these for garnish). Cook until just tender and lightly browned, 3 minutes, stirring with the side of the spatula. Note: If the vegetables remain too hard, squirt a tablespoon or two of water over them. It will boil when it hits the hot metal, steaming the veggies. Repeat as needed.

5. If using a protein, add it now and cook until seared on the outside and almost cooked through (in the case of the shrimp), 2 to 4 minutes.

6. Add the rice and cook it until hot, stirring and chopping with the side of the spatula so it and the vegetables cook evenly, 3 to 5 minutes. Halfway through, add the soy sauce and butter, and continue cooking until the butter melts and sizzles.

7. Work in the scrambled egg, again chopping and stirring with the side of the spatula. Cook until the rice is hot. Taste for seasoning, adding salt and pepper as needed—the fried rice should be highly seasoned.

8. Serve the fried rice hot off your griddle or transfer to a platter for serving. Sprinkle with the reserved scallion greens.

WHAT ELSE For the best results, use rice that's a day old. (Fresh rice gets mushy.) I've made this with Japanese haku mai (white rice), Thai jasmine rice, Indian basmati, and good old American Carolina-style rice. Some people add a little MSG to boost the umami flavor. Keep the cooked rice refrigerated until 1 hour before preparing.

WHAT'S MORE Fried rice is more a process than a recipe, and the variations are almost endless. A Chinese American–inspired version might include diced napa cabbage and mung bean sprouts (½ cup/70 g each). In addition to the soy sauce, add 1 tablespoon each rice wine and toasted sesame oil, plus 2 to 3 tablespoons chili crisp. (Chili crisp is a Chinese condiment made with fried chilies, onion, garlic, peanuts, MSG, salt, and a little sugar.) Look for it at Asian markets and many supermarkets or order it online. It will quickly become your new favorite ingredient!

For a version with Thai flavors, add 1 to 2 minced Thai chilies or other hot peppers to the aromatics. Substitute fish sauce for the soy sauce and add freshly grated lime zest (½ teaspoon), fresh lime juice (1 tablespoon), plus sugar (1 tablespoon). Top with 3 tablespoons chopped toasted peanuts.

CHAR SIU TOFU
(CHINESE BARBECUE STYLE)

SERVES 2 (CAN BE MULTIPLIED AS DESIRED)

If ever there was a protein expressly designed for the griddle, it's tofu. Fragile by nature, it won't fall apart on the griddle, and the hot flat metal fosters flavor-boosting browning. In this recipe, tofu gets the char siu (Chinese barbecue) treatment, with an irresistible sweet-salty-aromatic marinade you boil down into a savory glaze. That faint whiff of licorice? It comes from the star anise in the five spice powder.

1 package (14 to 16 ounces/395 to 455 g) extra-firm tofu

FOR THE MARINADE/GLAZE

3 tablespoons brown sugar (light or dark—your choice)

3 tablespoons soy sauce

2 tablespoons hoisin sauce, plus more for serving

2 tablespoons oyster sauce

2 tablespoons Chinese rice wine or sake

1 tablespoon toasted sesame oil, plus more for the griddle

½ teaspoon Chinese five spice powder

1 scallion, trimmed, white part smashed with the side of a cleaver, green part thinly sliced on the diagonal

TO SERVE (OPTIONAL)

8 steamed buns (see What Else), small brioche buns, or Hawaiian buns

1 cucumber, peeled and thinly sliced

8 radishes, scrubbed and thinly sliced or julienned

YOU'LL ALSO NEED

A large aluminum foil pan

1. Cut the tofu in half through the narrow side, then cut each half in half widthwise. You should have 4 tofu rectangles. Place them on an inclined cutting board (raise one end on a small measuring cup) and have the other end hanging over the sink. Place a second cutting board on top of the tofu. Press the tofu for 20 minutes to wring out the excess liquid.

2. Meanwhile, make the marinade. Combine the sugar, soy sauce, hoisin sauce, oyster sauce, rice wine, sesame oil, and five spice powder in the aluminum foil pan and whisk to mix.

(recipe continues)

(Tilt the pan to facilitate whisking.) Add the scallion whites and tofu and marinate, covered and in the refrigerator, for 2 hours, turning several times.

3. When ready to cook, heat your griddle or plancha to medium-high with one zone on high. Oil the medium-high zone well with sesame oil.

4. Gently remove the tofu pieces from the marinade (reserve the marinade) and arrange them on the griddle. Cook until sizzling and browned, 2 to 4 minutes per side. Don't let them burn.

5. Meanwhile, place the aluminum foil pan with the remaining marinade on the hot part of the griddle. Boil the marinade until it's reduced to a syrupy glaze, 2 to 4 minutes.

6. To serve simply: Transfer the tofu to a platter or plates and spoon the glaze over it. Sprinkle with the reserved scallion greens.

To serve more elaborately: If using steamed buns, wrap them in foil individually and warm for a minute on the griddle next to the tofu. If using brioche or Hawaiian buns, toast them, cut side down, on the griddle in a little sesame oil. Slice the tofu, place on the bun, and drizzle with some of the char siu glaze. Add the cucumber and radish slices and scallion greens and you're ready for tofu awesomeness!

WHAT ELSE Choose extra-firm tofu when possible. Pressing it extracts some of the water and makes it even firmer. Hoisin sauce is a dark, sweet, salty condiment made from soybeans. (I think of it as the Chinese version of ketchup.) Oyster sauce is a salty, briny condiment rich in umami flavors. Five spice powder owes its sweet spice flavor to cinnamon and star anise. Steamed buns are available frozen at Asian markets and many supermarkets. Otherwise, use brioche hamburger buns.

WHAT'S MORE This char siu marinade/glaze makes just about everything taste amazing: griddled fish, shrimp, chicken, pork, vegetables—you name it.

This tofu recipe rocks, but it's not the only one we make at our house. Barbecued tofu is another Raichlen family standby: Cut and press the tofu as directed above and brush with olive oil or melted butter. Generously sprinkle both sides with your favorite barbecue rub. (I'm partial to my Kansas City Smoke Rub.) Griddle as directed above. Toast 4 brioche buns, cut side down, on the griddle. Serve the tofu on the buns with lettuce, sliced tomato, sweet pickle slices, and your favorite barbecue sauce. Sliced cheese and sliced onions are optional.

Griddle Feast

A TEPPAN YAKI DINNER

Griddles are found around the world, of course, but no one turns them into performance art like the Japanese. Visit a Japanese-style steakhouse, like Benihana or Samurai, for edible proof. The teppan (as the griddle is known in Japan) serves not only to cook your dinner, but as the table off which you eat it; the chef (in this case, you) doubles as the host and the meal becomes an evening's entertainment. On page 174 you can read about my own adventures as a Benihana chef. Don't worry about cutting an egg in half in midair with your spatula. Concentrate on preparing the following and let the party begin.

Here's what's on the menu:

- Fried Rice and Company (page 223)
- Teppan Yaki Zucchini (page 216)
- Onion Volcano (page 219)
- Teppan Yaki Shrimp (page 193)

Here's how to sequence the preparation:

The night before:
- Cook and cool the rice. Refrigerate it.

Before the meal prep:
- Chop the vegetables and aromatics for the fried rice.
- Slice the zucchini and onions.
- Peel and devein the shrimp.

- Measure out and assemble the ingredients for the other dishes on trays.

The actual cook:
- Heat your griddle or plancha with one zone on high, one on medium-high, and one on medium-low. Oil the griddle.

- Prepare and serve the fried rice. Cook on the medium-high zone.

- While cooking the rice, start the zucchini. Cook the zucchini on the high zone. Serve when ready.

- Prepare and serve the onion volcano. Cook on the medium-high and medium-low zones.

- Prepare and serve the shrimp. Cook on the medium-high zone.

CHAPTER 10

DESSERTS

Okay. You know how to griddle dirty eggs (page 31) and Smash Browns (page 209). You know how to sizzle a cheesesteak (page 81) and cook an A5 Wagyu (page 140). You appreciate the wonders a plancha can work on seafood (pages 183–201) and you've mastered teppan yaki fried rice (page 223). Your last challenge is dessert. Most North Americans don't think of dessert on the griddle, but elsewhere on Planet Plancha, griddled desserts are a big deal. Take France, for example, where crêpes turn up both at street corner stalls and Michelin-starred restaurants. (Suzette, anyone?) Or Spain, where torrijas (wine-soaked French toast) is a traditional Easter dessert. And speaking of French toast, it was featured in one of the "Mystery Box" segments on my *Project Smoke* TV show, in which I lift a box to reveal a surprise ingredient for which I create a recipe on the spot in real time. A loaf of brioche was the ingredient in this case: I used it to make chocolate banana brioche toast on a griddle. Learn how to make it here.

BURNT PEACHES
WITH SOUR CREAM AND BROWN SUGAR

SERVES 4

It's hard to improve on a luscious ripe peach eaten at the height of summer. But I'm going to try. The secret is—you guessed it—a griddle. In a nutshell, you dredge peach halves in brown sugar, which you caramelize in butter on screaming hot metal. This "burns" the sugar to a candy crust. The resulting smoky caramel flavor goes great with the brassy, musky taste of peach. To finish it off is a fragrant sweet-tart topping made with sour cream, cardamom, and brown sugar.

---

4 large ripe luscious peaches, preferably freestone

3 tablespoons cold unsalted butter in a chunk for the griddle

1 cup (145 g) dark brown sugar (light or dark—your choice), in a shallow bowl, plus more for serving

½ cup (120 g) sour cream

Ground cinnamon or cardamom for sprinkling (optional)

---

1. Cut the peaches in half through the crease (the ridge running around half the circumference of the fruit). Cut to the stone, then twist the halves in opposite directions to separate them. They'll come apart easily in a freestone peach; you'll have to do some whittling on a clingstone. Discard the stone.

2. Meanwhile, heat your griddle or plancha to high. Impale the chunk of butter on a fork and rub the butter on the griddle in an section just large enough to hold the peach halves.

3. Dip the cut side of each peach in brown sugar, twisting it to coat the bottom. Immediately transfer the peach halves to the griddle, placing them coated side down. Cook until the bottom is sizzling, browned, and caramelized, 2 to 3 minutes. If you get it right, the bottom will be caramelized and the flesh under the rounded half will remain raw.

4. Transfer the peaches, caramelized side up, to a platter or plates. Top each with a dollop of sour cream and a spoonful of brown sugar. If you're so inclined, a sprinkling of cinnamon or cardamom takes an amazing dessert over the top.

(recipe continues)

WHAT ELSE The recipe takes all of 5 minutes to assemble, but it does require you to walk a razor's edge between caramelized (good) and burnt (not so good). For ease in handling, buy freestone, not clingstone peaches: The former separate into halves easily. With clingstone peaches, cut in half to the pit as you would an avocado, then using a paring knife, whittle out the stone. It's virtually impossible to buy ripe peaches these days—especially at the supermarket. Ripen them in a paper bag until gently yielding and very fragrant, 1 to 4 days.

WHAT'S MORE The method outlined in the recipe works great with all ripe stone fruit, from nectarines and apricots to plums. I call for sour cream here, but crème fraîche (a tart French-style sour cream), Mexican crema, fresh ricotta, or even whipped cream work equally well. For that matter, you could serve the peaches with peach or vanilla ice cream.

PEPPERED PINEAPPLE
WITH MEZCAL WHIPPED CREAM

SERVES 4

Grilled pineapple has been part of my repertoire since I wrote *The Barbecue! Bible*. So how does the preparation translate to the griddle? I'm delighted to report that you get the same smoky-sweet caramelization, the same succulent flesh—with a lot less risk of flare-ups. In the following recipe, black pepper cranks up the heat, while mezcal adds the smoke.

FOR THE MEZCAL WHIPPED CREAM

¾ cup (180 ml) heavy (whipping) cream

2 tablespoons confectioners' sugar

2 tablespoons mezcal, or to taste

FOR THE PINEAPPLE

1 cup (200 g) granulated sugar

1 tablespoon freshly ground black pepper, or to taste

3 tablespoons butter (salted or unsalted— your call), melted, plus 2 tablespoons cold butter in a chunk for the griddle

1 pineapple, peeled, cored, and cut crosswise into ½-inch-thick (1 cm) slices

YOU'LL ALSO NEED

A shallow bowl or aluminum foil pan

1. Make the whipped cream: Place the cream in a chilled bowl and beat with an electric mixer until it starts to thicken, 3 to 5 minutes. Add the confectioners' sugar and mezcal and continue beating to soft peaks, 2 to 4 minutes more. The whipped cream can be prepared several hours ahead and kept, covered, in the refrigerator.

2. Just before serving, heat your griddle or plancha to high.

3. Prepare the pineapple: Combine the granulated sugar and pepper in a shallow bowl or aluminum foil pan and stir to mix. Have this mixture by the side of the griddle.

4. Impale the chunk of butter on a fork and rub it on the griddle to grease it.

(recipe continues)

5. Brush the pineapple slices on both sides with the melted butter. Using tongs or a fork, dip each pineapple slice in the sugar mixture to coat both sides, shaking off the excess. As you coat the pineapple slices, place them on the griddle.

6. Cook the pineapple slices until sizzling and darkly browned on the bottom, 2 to 4 minutes. Using a spatula, invert and cook the other side the same way.

7. Transfer the pineapple slices to a platter or plates and top with dollops of the mezcal whipped cream.

WHAT ELSE When buying whole pineapple, look for fruit with a yellow or golden rind: It will be sweeter than those with green rinds. To save time, you could use prepeeled and precored pineapple. Again, a bright yellow color indicates sweetness. Slice crosswise as directed. Mezcal is a Mexican cactus spirit with a pronounced smoky flavor—the result of roasting agave hearts in a fire-heated pit.

CARAMELIZED PEARS
WITH CHOCOLATE AND ALMONDS (A NEW PEARS BELLE HÉLÈNE)

MAKES 4 HALVES, SERVES 2 TO 4

Pears Belle Hélène (created by the legendary French chef Escoffier and named for an opera by Offenbach) was one of the first desserts I learned to make at La Varenne, the cooking school in Paris. This combination of sweet pears, bitter chocolate sauce, nutty toasted almonds, and suave vanilla ice cream is universal in its appeal. Like all great desserts—like all great dishes—the whole is greater than the sum of the parts. I've reimagined this French classic on the griddle, caramelizing the pears in cinnamon sugar and butter.

FOR THE PEARS

2 very ripe sweet, fragrant pears, scrubbed and stemmed

¾ cup (150 g) sugar

2 teaspoons ground cinnamon

½ cup (55 g) slivered almonds

2 tablespoons cold unsalted butter in a chunk for the griddle

FOR SERVING

1 cup (225 g) vanilla ice cream

Bittersweet Chocolate Sauce (recipe follows)

YOU'LL ALSO NEED

A small aluminum foil pan or shallow dish

1. Cut each pear in half lengthwise and remove the seeds and core. Cut a ¼-inch (6 mm) slice off each rounded side so the pear halves sit steady.

2. Place the sugar in a small aluminum foil pan or shallow dish. Stir in the cinnamon.

3. Heat your griddle or plancha to high, with one zone on medium-high.

4. Arrange the almonds on the medium-high zone of the griddle and toast until golden brown, 2 minutes, turning with a spatula. Transfer to a bowl to cool.

5. Impale the butter on a fork and rub the butter over the hot section of the griddle. Using tongs, dip each pear half in the cinnamon sugar on all of the cut sides, shaking off the excess. Arrange the pears, flat side down, on the buttered section of the plancha and cook until darkly caramelized, 2 minutes or as needed. Invert the pears and caramelize the rounded part the same way. Transfer the pear halves to plates or bowls.

6. Top each pear with a scoop of ice cream, followed by a drizzle of chocolate sauce and the toasted almonds. Serve at once.

WHAT ELSE To get the full effect of this recipe, the pears must be fragrant and soft, meaning you'll likely need to ripen them at room temperature for a few days before preparing this dish. The French would use a comice or Bartlett pear, but any fragrant ripe pear will do.

BITTERSWEET CHOCOLATE SAUCE

MAKES 1¼ CUPS (295 ML)

For the best results, use chocolate that is 65 percent cocoa beans or more. This may make more chocolate sauce than you need for two pears. In my book, it's always good to have a little leftover for future use.

½ cup (120 ml) heavy (whipping) cream

1 cup (6 ounces/170 g) chopped semisweet or bittersweet chocolate

½ teaspoon pure vanilla extract

Bring the heavy cream to a boil in a small saucepan. Stir in the chocolate and vanilla. Heat just enough to melt the chocolate, 2 to 4 minutes. Use immediately while still warm.

TORRIJAS
(SPANISH "FRENCH" TOAST)

SERVES 4

Torrijas has been described as Spanish French toast, but it differs from the North American version in several key ways. First, it often contains wine, which gives the toast an interesting sweet-tart finish. Second, it's often flavored with finely grated orange or lemon zest, adding pleasing citrus notes. It's customary to fry it in olive oil, not butter. Finally, it's traditionally served at Easter—not for breakfast but dessert. Some people drizzle it with honey; others sprinkle it with confectioners' sugar or cinnamon sugar. Being a more-is-more kind of guy, I use both.

Eight ¾-inch-thick (2 cm) slices of brioche, country-style white bread, or baguette (if using the latter, slice it on the diagonal), ideally a little stale

5 large eggs (preferably organic)

1 teaspoon pure vanilla extract

½ teaspoon freshly and finely grated orange zest, grated on a Microplane

½ teaspoon freshly and finely grated lemon zest (or more orange zest), grated on a Microplane

2 cups (480 ml) half-and-half

¾ cup (180 ml) sweet wine, like Malaga, or dry or cream sherry (or more half-and-half)

¾ cup (150 g) sugar

1 tablespoon ground cinnamon

¼ teaspoon ground cloves

Extra virgin olive oil for the griddle

Honey or maple syrup for drizzling (optional)

---

1. Arrange the bread slices in a single layer in a baking dish just large enough to accommodate them without overlapping. Place the eggs, vanilla, and orange and lemon zest in a mixing bowl and whisk until smooth. Whisk in the half-and-half and wine. Pour this mixture over the bread slices, turning to coat both sides. Soak the bread until soft, 10 minutes.

2. Combine the sugar, cinnamon, and ground cloves in a small bowl and mix with a fork. Set aside for serving.

3. Meanwhile, heat your griddle or plancha to medium-high. Oil it well with olive oil. Arrange the soaked bread slices on the hot metal, leaving 1 inch (3 cm) or so between them. Cook until browned on the bottom, 2 to 4 minutes.

4. Drizzle more oil on the griddle and invert the bread slices on top. Cook until the bread is cooked through and browned on the bottom, another 2 to 4 minutes.

5. Transfer the torrijas to a warmed platter or plates. Dust with the cinnamon-clove sugar or drizzle with honey (or both).

WHAT ELSE The addition of wine to the batter makes torrijas unique among French toasts. But which wine you use depends on where you're from. If you come from southeastern Spain, you'd likely use a dark, sweet, fortified wine called Malaga. If you come from the Cádiz region, you'd probably use sherry. If you want to skip the alcohol, just add more half-and-half.

WHAT'S MORE Mexico has a unique twist on torrijas: caballeros pobres (literally, "poor horsemen"). Start with sliced bread soaked in the egg and milk mixture from the recipe, but spice it with cinnamon, cloves, and a pinch of nutmeg instead of citrus zest. Cook the bread on the griddle, then steep it in a raisin-studded brown sugar syrup (1 part brown sugar to 2 parts water, plus a handful of dark raisins—boil for 3 minutes, then cool to room temperature). Serve caballeros pobres in a shallow bowl with plenty of syrup and raisins spooned over it. I wouldn't say no to some toasted slivered almonds on top.

CHOCOLATE BANANA FRENCH TOAST

SERVES 4

One of the most popular features on my *Project Fire* TV show was our "Mystery Box" segment. I would walk onto the set to find a large wooden box. Under it was a surprise ingredient, and my challenge was to create a recipe using it in real time. In the past, I've found such random ingredients as giant squid, frog legs, chicken livers, and even sunflowers, and I love the spontaneity of coming up with a recipe to grill them. One Mystery Box was particularly memorable in that it featured a loaf of bread. Not just any bread, but that gorgeous egg- and butter-rich bread the French call brioche—made by one of our prep chefs, Rebecca Dubis. To round out the recipe, I raided our "pantry"—a sort of shopping cart where I gather auxiliary supplies to accompany the mystery ingredient. Here I found chocolate, bananas, brandy, eggs, and heavy cream. The mandate was clear: I'd make chocolate banana French toast. This particular segment was filmed late at night, and the crew loved the combination of bread, chocolate, and bananas built into a sandwich as much as I did—especially when theatrically flambéed with rum.

FOR THE FRENCH TOAST

1 loaf of brioche bread

6 large eggs (preferably organic)

2 cups (480 ml) heavy (whipping) cream or half-and-half

1 teaspoon ground cinnamon

1 teaspoon pure vanilla extract

Pinch of coarse salt (sea or kosher)

TO FINISH AND SERVE

2 ripe bananas, peeled and thinly sliced crosswise

1 cup (6 ounces/170 g) dark chocolate chips

Canola or olive oil for the griddle

4 tablespoons (55 g) unsalted butter, cut into 8 slices

½ cup (40 g) toasted shaved coconut (optional, see What Else)

¼ cup (60 ml) dark rum (optional)

YOU'LL ALSO NEED

A long-handled match or butane match (optional)

(recipe continues)

1. Cut the brioche into eight ½-inch-thick (1 cm) slices. (Save the heels and remaining bread for another use.)

2. Crack the eggs into a mixing bowl and whisk to mix. Whisk in the cream, cinnamon, vanilla, and salt. Pour half the batter into a nonreactive baking dish—it should be just large and deep enough to accommodate 4 sandwiches without overlapping.

3. Lay 4 slices of brioche in the batter and top evenly with the sliced bananas, then chocolate chips. Top with the remaining slices of brioche and pour the remaining batter evenly over the top of the sandwiches. Let the bread soak for 20 minutes.

4. Heat your griddle or plancha to medium and lightly oil it.

5. Place 4 slices of the butter on the griddle, spacing them 6 inches (15 cm) apart. Using a spatula, carefully transfer the French toast sandwiches to the griddle and place atop the butter. Cook until golden brown on the bottom, 3 to 6 minutes. Working with 1 sandwich at a time, slide a spatula underneath, lift it, and place a pat of butter on the griddle underneath; when it melts, carefully invert the French toast sandwich on top of it and cook until golden brown, 3 to 6 minutes.

6. Transfer the French toast sandwiches to a fire-proof platter or plates. Sprinkle with toasted coconut, if using.

7. Warm the rum to body temperature (tepid) in small saucepan. Do not let it boil. Carefully light it with a long-handled match and pour the flaming rum over the French toast. Serve as the flames die down.

WHAT ELSE French brioche is firmer than what passes for brioche in the US. You need a firm brioche (if too soft, the French toast will be mushy). Alternatively, use a firm country-style white bread.

To toast the coconut for the top, spread the chips on the medium-high zone of your griddle (make sure the cook-top is clean and dry). Cook until lightly browned, turning with a spatula, 1 to 2 minutes. Immediately transfer to a bowl to cool.

WHAT'S MORE For most Americans, French toast means breakfast, but elsewhere in the world, it's eaten as dessert. In Spain, for example, French toast takes the form of torrijas (page 238)—bread soaked in an egg and wine batter and drizzled with honey for dessert.

CRÊPES AND CO.

MAKES 9 TO 12 CRÊPES (8 INCHES/20 CM EACH)

Visit a crêperie in France (they're as common as burger joints are in the US), and you'll find a piece of cooking equipment perfectly suited to crêpe making. It's a crêpière, a perfectly round gas-heated griddle 15 to 20 inches (38 to 50 cm) across. You pour batter onto it, spreading it into a perfect circle with a tiny rake. A minute or so per side, and your crêpe is ready. Here's a rich, buttery crêpe batter I learned to make at the La Varenne cooking school in Paris years ago—still a Raichlen family favorite.

FOR THE CRÊPES

3 large eggs (preferably organic), beaten with a fork

1½ cups (355 ml) whole milk

½ teaspoon coarse salt (sea or kosher)

½ teaspoon sugar

1 cup (125 g) flour

4 tablespoons (55 g) unsalted butter, melted

Vegetable oil or melted butter to oil the griddle

FOR FILLING

Unsalted butter, at room temperature

Sugar

Fresh lemon and/or orange for squeezing (optional)

---

1. Make the batter: Combine the eggs, milk, salt, sugar, and flour in a blender and blend to a smooth batter. Work in the melted butter. Blend just to mix—a minute will do it.

2. Heat your griddle or plancha to medium. Lightly grease the griddle with oil or melted butter (wipe it on with a paper towel). Try not to leave visible pools of fat.

3. Pour the crêpe batter onto the griddle ⅓ cup (80 ml) at a time.

Using a crêpe rake or your spatula, spread it into 8-inch (20 cm) circles. Cook until the bottom is brown and small beads of butter form on the top, 1 minute. Using a metal spatula, flip the crêpes and cook the other side the same way.

4. The simplest dessert crêpe comes smeared with unsalted butter and sprinkled with sugar. (My editor, Kylie Foxx McDonald, likes to add a squeeze of fresh lemon and/or orange juice.) Fold it in quarters and serve.

(recipe continues)

WHAT ELSE I suggest making your crêpe batter in a blender. That way, it's easy to pour the precise amount onto your griddle. If not, use a large measuring cup or pitcher. Crêpe rakes are available at cookware shops and on Amazon. Alternatively, use a spatula or the back of a large metal spoon for spreading the batter. It may take some practice to achieve crêpes that are perfectly round. Don't worry—whatever their shape, they'll still taste awesome. Note: As the crêpe batter sits, it thickens, so thin it with additional milk as needed—it should have the consistency of heavy cream.

WHAT'S MORE This classic butter-and-sugar-filled crêpe is a favorite of French schoolchildren everywhere, and what I like about it is that you can really taste the crêpe. (Unlike a Nutella crêpe, in which all you taste is the Nutella.) But feel free to spread the crêpe with your favorite jam, crème de marron (sweetened chestnut puree), or of course, Nutella.

Among the more popular savory versions in France is the ham, egg, and cheese crêpe. Cook the crêpe on one side. Flip it and crack an egg in the center. Sprinkle the top with diced ham (brown a thin slice of ham on the griddle, then cut it into ½-inch/1 cm squares). Add a generous handful of coarsely grated Gruyère cheese. Cook under a griddle dome until the egg is done to taste, 3 to 5 minutes for sunny-side up. Fold it in quarters and serve.

RESOURCES

GRIDDLES, GRILL INSERTS, PLANCHAS

Arteflame (Arteflame.com)
Round freestanding grill and griddle hybrids, griddle inserts for select charcoal and gas grill models, griddle accessories

Big Green Egg (Biggreenegg.com)
Griddle inserts

Blackstone (Blackstoneproducts.com)
Freestanding griddles, portable tabletop griddles, cabinet-style griddles, indoor griddles, griddle accessories

Camp Chef (Campchef.com)
Freestanding gas griddles, griddle accessories

Cuisinart (Cuisinart.com)
Round freestanding gas griddles, griddle accessories

Evo (Evoamerica.com)
Residential and commercial flattop griddles (gas and electric) for indoor / outdoor use

Hancock Grills (Hancockgrills.com)
Fire bowl–style wood-burning griddles

Lodge Cast Iron (Lodgecastiron.com)
Portable cast iron and carbon-steel griddles

Made In (Madeincookware.com)
Portable griddles, griddle accessories

OFYR (Ofyr.com)
Bowl-style stand-alone wood-burning griddles

OnlyFire (Onlyfire.com)
Portable tabletop portable gas griddles

Pit Boss (Pitboss-grills.com)
Gas outdoor griddles, portable tabletop griddles

Royal Gourmet (Royalgourmetusa.com)
Freestanding grill and griddle hybrids, portable tabletop griddles

Sophia & William (Sophia-william.com)
Freestanding gas griddles

Steven Raichlen Signature Series (Amazon.com)
Portable plancha

Traeger (Traeger.com)
Freestanding gas griddles

Weber (Weber.com)
Freestanding gas griddles, griddle inserts for Weber gas grills

SPECIALTY FOODS

Asian ingredients
Sayweee.com

Cheese
Igourmet.com

Grape must syrup (saba)
Amazon.com

Italian ingredients
Bellaitaliafoodstore.com

Latin American ingredients
Amigofoods.com

Maple syrup
Runamokmaple.com

Middle Eastern ingredients
Mideastgrocers.com

Spanish ingredients
Tienda.com

Specialty produce
Melissas.com

Spices
Burlapandbarrel.com

INDEX

Page number in *italics* indicate photographs.

ACKNOWLEDGMENTS

The most fun part of writing a book is thanking the people who helped make it happen.

On the home front: Barbara, Ella, Mia, Julian, Betsy, and Jake.

At Workman Publishing: Kylie Foxx McDonald, Analucia Zepeda, Becky Terhune, Kate Karol, Julia Perry, Barbara Peragine, Carol White, Jessica Easto, Anne Wright, Suzanne Fass, Lori Newhouse, Vivian Wick, Rebecca Carlisle, Allison McGeehon, Chloe Puton, Moira Kerrigan, and Lia Ronnen.

At barbecuebible.com: Daniel Hale, John White, Jared Reiter, Steve Nestor.

The Barbecue Bible 500 Club and test kitchen: Alynne and Robbie Douglass, Frank and Kelley DeTuro, Sam and Charlene Swanlund, and Dax Turner.

And a special thanks to: José Andrés, Maria Antonieta Garcia, Elvin Perez, Craig Reed, Kristina Peterson-Lohman at Weber-Stephen Products LLC, and especially my heroic assistant, Nancy Loseke!

ABOUT THE AUTHOR

 **STEVEN RAICHLEN** is an author, journalist, lecturer, TV host, and the man who launched the barbecue revolution. He hosts some of the most engaging cooking shows on Public Television, from his new Planet Barbecue® series, which explores global grilling, to his perennially popular *Project Fire*, *Project Smoke*, and *Primal Grill*. Raichlen stars in several French-language TV shows, including *Le Maître du Grill* and an Italian TV show on Gambero Rosso called *Steven Raichlen Grills Italy*.

Steven Raichlen has written thirty-three books, including the international blockbusters *The Barbecue! Bible* and *How to Grill* (each million-plus copy bestsellers) and the *New York Times* bestselling *Planet Barbecue* and *Project Smoke*. Raichlen's books have won five James Beard Awards; three IACP Julia Child Awards, and have been translated into seventeen languages. He's a member of the Barbecue Hall of Fame and Taste Awards Hall of Fame.

An award-winning journalist, Raichlen writes for the *New York Times*. His work has been featured in the *Wall Street Journal*, *Esquire*, *GQ*, and all the major food magazines. He has appeared on major TV and radio shows in the US and abroad, from *Oprah* and the *Today Show* to *Fresh Air with Terry Gross* and *Howard Stern*. He also battled—and defeated—the Iron Chef in a Battle of the Barbecue Gods on Japanese television.

Raichlen founded Barbecue University®, a unique cooking school held at the Alisal Ranch in Solvang, California—hailed as "A fantasy camp for coal heads" (*Cooking Light Magazine*) and the #1 barbecue experience in the United States (The Food Network). A lively speaker with decades of experience, Raichlen has lectured at institutions as varied as Harvard University, the National Press Club, and the Smithsonian Institution.

Raichlen's latest ventures are a restaurant concept—the Star Grill by Steven Raichlen—for the Windstar cruise line and a line of prepared, ready-to-heat-and-eat barbecue called Planet Barbecue®.

Steven Raichlen holds a degree in French literature from Reed College in Portland, Oregon, and studied medieval cooking in Europe on a Thomas J. Watson Foundation Fellowship. He was also awarded a Fulbright. When not grilling, you'll find him at the helm of his sailboat, *Barbacoa*. He and his wife, Barbara, live in Miami, Florida, and Martha's Vineyard, Massachusetts.